THE AMERICAN SCHOOLBOOK

By the same author

THEY SHALL NOT PASS

THE WATCHDOGS OF WALL STREET

BUY NOW, PAY LATER

THE THIEF IN THE WHITE COLLAR
   (*with Norman Jaspan*)

THE ROYAL VULTURES
   (*with Sam Kolman*)

HILLEL BLACK

THE
AMERICAN
SCHOOLBOOK

WILLIAM MORROW & COMPANY, INC.

NEW YORK

1967

For Granny

Contents

At a Harvard School of Education Seminar for publishers recently, a group of us took our lumps, and perhaps deservedly, for being too timid. HEW Secretary John Gardner's comment at the recent White House Conference that the great problems of education should now be attacked with the "bold bite of a barracuda" was repeated, with the hint that we educational editors might be only piranha fish or, even worse, ordinary flounders.

While I must loyally deny such jibes, I do suspect that we publishers have sometimes been less receptive to fresh, new educational ideas than we might have been, and than we must be in the future. As a young editor—which was far too many years ago—I had two publishing maxims painstakingly pounded into me, and I imagine that most of my colleagues here did too.

The first was that the most damaging publishing mistakes are made by investing heavily in good ideas—not bad ideas, mind you, but good ones—that are too far ahead of their time.

The second mistake is even worse. It is the mortal sin of publishing. This sin is for a publisher to delude himself with the notion that he knows better than professional educators what materials are best for schools to use. "You are the service guy behind the cafeteria counter. Your job is to supply the customer with what he wants, not the dietitian telling him what he should have for dinner."

These maxims are, I think, still generally valid. I doubt seriously whether publishers are likely to become much bolder or more experimental than the educators they serve.

—LYLE M. SPENCER, President of Science Research Associates, a Subsidiary of I.B.M., in a speech before the American Textbook Publishers Institute and the Great Cities Research Council, November, 1965.

CHAPTER *1*

The Importance of Textbooks

Miss MABEL O'DONNELL, a successful author of children's textbooks, begins her working day in a cramped study in her six-room ranch-style home in Aurora, Illinois. There, promptly at nine in the morning, this shy, matronly woman enters a never-never world filled with talking owls, chattering squirrels, and the antics of a red-haired girl named Janet and her blond, brown-eyed brother, Mark. On this day Miss O'Donnell, using a standard typewriter set on a mahogany desk, began composing "A Bad Morning."

Mark was as cross as a bear.
When a boy is that cross,
he is just as cross
as a boy can get.
If you are wise,
you will look out
for someone like that.

As the story tumbled onto the 5½-by-8-inch sheet of paper, Miss O'Donnell solved a number of technical writing problems that few other authors ever face. In this tale, which will be used in schools to teach six-year-olds to read, she employed words no longer than two syllables in length and introduced at the most only one new word to a page. Despite the limited vocabulary, every sentence and paragraph had to flow smoothly, and her plot had to prove so imaginative and universal in theme that a child in the suburbs, a youngster in the slums, and a farmer's son would each feel compelled to read more. Finally, Miss O'Donnell had taken it upon herself to design each page as she wrote, so that every line would be printed and published almost exactly as it came out of her typewriter. The fact that Mabel O'Donnell can do all this on demand and to perfection makes her one of the highest paid, most successful authors in the history of publishing.

As the creator of the Janet and Mark books and before that Alice and Jerry, a first-through-sixth-grade reading series second only to Dick and Jane in popularity, Miss O'Donnell has earned over $2,700,000 in royalties, according to Harper & Row, her publisher. Since 1936, when Alice and Jerry first appeared, over 67 million copies of her books have been sold in hardcover, more than the total United States sales of all the books written by Ian Fleming. (Ironically, she was once told by a University of Chicago creative-writing teacher that she would never make any money as an author.) Over the past three decades more than 300 million children have read Miss O'Donnell's books, which means that this former grade-school teacher from Aurora has probably had more influence on what young children learn than any other single, living American. Not only do her books continue to teach millions of children to read, but they also serve as their main source of literature and homilies such as honesty, perseverance, and self-denial.

"Oh, Father," says Jerry in the first-grade reader, "I want the ball. I want the boat. I want the train."

Father firmly replies, "You may have just one toy, Jerry. Just one toy."

"One toy! One toy!" says Jerry.

Despite her extraordinary impact on the minds of children and her influence on what takes place in classrooms throughout the country, few parents have ever heard of Mabel O'Donnell or examined the textbooks she has written. In a similar fashion, few people are aware of the important role some 250 million textbooks play in the education of 50,000,000 elementary and high-school students. For instance, during his school career your child will either commit to memory or attempt to absorb at least 32,000 textbook pages, and this does not include supplementary readings in social studies, literature, or science. In the first grade he will complete at least four textbooks, and by the time he finishes his last year in high school, he will intensely study another sixty. These books impart most of the skills and knowledge he will learn in school, covering every subject from beginning reading and arithmetic to high-school biology, physics, economics, algebra, French, American history, and literature. During the school day itself, 75 percent of your child's classroom time and at night 90 percent of the time he spends on homework will be centered around textbooks.

"Textbooks," declared *School Management*, a magazine published for school administrators and school-board members, "are still the single most important teaching tool. Put all your new teaching tools together—the projectors, the films, the teaching machines—and they're just a drop in the bucket compared to that old stand-by, the textbook. Invariably, the textbook is the basis of every curriculum. To an overwhelming extent, it determines what will be taught and when."

The textbook and its even heftier manual also will determine *how* almost any given subject will be taught. The teacher's textbook or manual which accompanies your youngster's schoolbook is given to all classroom instructors who use the publisher's materials. The teacher's guide is frequently more elaborate than the children's text, containing every word and illustration in your youngster's text plus an extensive explanation of what your child will read and study. Moreover, the teacher's manual organizes the course for the teacher, describes most of the teaching techniques she will use, and provides hundreds of student homework assignments, discussion and test questions, as well as the answers.

The teacher's manuals supplied by Mabel O'Donnell illustrate the extent to which the textbook and its guide can dominate classroom teaching in America. For instance, the four pre-primers in the Alice and Jerry series contain a total of 236 pages, but her teacher's guide boasts 528 pages. In the manual she offers instructions on how to teach not only each page but each word in the pre-primers. She even supplies complete scripts the teacher can read aloud to the class. For example, a first-grade teacher who is about to teach the initial consonant "s" sound simply turns to page eighty-five in the manual and reads aloud:

"I hope your bright eyes are working this morning. I hope you can—(put *see* in the card holder and have it read). Say the word softly with me. Do you hear how *see* begins? (Trace the *s* with your finger.) Grandmother *sent* Alice a cap. *Sent-see!* What did you discover?" Although high-school manuals are less detailed, they usually explain every passage in the text to the teacher and they frequently provide the equivalent of a year's college course on how to teach the subject.

Despite the fact that publishers usually list and encourage teachers to use outside readings, most teachers rarely wander far from the guides or texts. Dr. Ruth G. Strickland, professor of education at Indiana University, estimates that about half the nation's primary teachers slavishly follow the guides. According to Dr. Bruce Joyce, the former head of elementary teacher education at the University of Chicago, about 80 percent of the nation's elementary teachers use textbooks as their main teaching tool and source of knowledge.

Dr. Joyce, associate professor of education at Teachers College, Columbia, has observed teachers at work in Delaware, Detroit, Chicago, and suburban New York. "The typical elementary teacher," he declares, "is called upon to master a range of subjects from children's literature to reading and from math to science. Since few people can become experts in so many fields, the typical grade-school teacher relies heavily on the texts and guides."

"There is probably an even greater reliance on textbooks in high school," Dr. Joyce adds. "Because the high-school teacher works with as many as 150 youngsters a day, it is impossible for him to prepare tailor-made materials for each child or even each class. He has to come up with the prepared package, the textbook."

This reporter's observations suggest that more often than not the American schoolteacher serves as an adult presence who is no wiser or better than the textbooks her children use. In Frank Jennings' apt description she "becomes an automatic playback machine," who does little more than echo the schoolbooks, the manuals, and guides passed on to her by an uninspired school administration. While it would be unfair to expect every teacher to be as searching as an Aristotle (and no doubt appalling to find every student a Plato), there may be some truth in the proposition that the professing art was first stricken by McGuffey's Eclectic Readers and interred in the manual to Dick and Jane.

In appearance at least the American textbook has few peers. Profusely illustrated, laid out in the same fashion as the mass consumer magazines, most schoolbooks are far more inviting than the textbooks used thirty years ago.* In contrast there has been little change in the actual content of nearly all history books, most readers, grammars, and civics books. Devoid of controversy, stylistically dull, they remain vacuous and boring. The wonder indeed is not that Johnny can read (despite the critics, the Dick and Janes do teach him how to read) but that Johnny, after a twelve-year diet of schoolbooks, wants to read at all.

At the same time one must temper such harsh comments with the hopeful observation that the textbook industry—and as a result American education—like the Devonian lungfish, is emerging from a dark and murky sea. For at long last one finds a multiplicity of revolutions taking place in the American schoolroom, changes which are being wrought by new textbooks and learning tools. Already affected are the sciences—physics, biology, chemistry, mathematics—and foreign languages. And now that the succulent teat of federal aid is available to all, even the social scientists and teachers of literature are displaying that kind of courage and individuality of thought that could cause an extraordinary improvement in the education of at least our children's children.

In sum, an examination of the workings of textbook publishing should offer some understanding of why American education has failed so many children and how and why the process of learning is finally becoming an exciting and meaningful venture. To get at the reasons for these failures and changes this book will investigate the various groups within and without the textbook industry who decide what shall and shall not be included in the nation's schoolbooks. It

---

* Some educators question whether these design changes are actually educational improvements. Like the addition of chrome and tail fins to cars, they may only distract both the child while learning and the teacher while she makes up her mind whether she should recommend the textbook for classroom use.

will attempt to show how and why a publisher decides to bring out a new textbook and the forces that go into choosing what information it will contain. This book also will describe textbook censorship at work and how a single state can determine some of the content of the schoolbooks your child may use. The reader will learn, too, how textbooks are written and sold and how schools select them. Finally, there will be an examination of some of the ways textbooks are changing and in turn revolutionizing grade- and high-school education.*

For the textbook publishers themselves this has become an era of transition and ferment. Until recently the antediluvians of education, they have had the modern age thrust upon them. As the creators or producers of the nation's teaching tools they must deal with the awesome knowledge explosion brought about by the splitting of the atom, the space age, the computer, and the onrushing step of history. As John I. Goodlad, professor of education at the University of California, Los Angeles, summed it up, "Beginning with the birth of Christ, it is estimated that the first doubling of knowledge occurred in 1750, the second in 1900, the third in 1950, and the fourth in 1960."

This flood of knowledge affects almost every subject. When Professor Jerrold Zacharias of M.I.T. and a group of eminent scientists recently prepared a new physics text for high-school students, they wrote that "some day" man will make a satellite that will go around the earth. "Within one year," Professor Zacharias recalled, "we had to strike that out." Recently a book salesman showed a revised American history text to his father who was astounded to discover that

---

* Censorship and other problems found in elementary and high-school publishing are less likely to arise in the college text field which is similar to trade book publishing. Hence, this examination concentrates on grade- and high-school textbooks and the industry that produces them.

one-third of the events described in the book had occurred since he attended high school.

Textbook publishers also face the difficult task of creating books that prepare both the poor who swell the city schools and the college-bound suburban child for economic survival in this age of rapid technological change. They must answer the urgent demands of the civil rights groups who call for integrated textbooks as well as integrated schools, and they must do business with those southern states who will only buy all-white editions. Moreover, they must adjust to the educational revolution brought on by the richly endowed, federally sponsored commissions and study groups which are creating their own radically different textbooks and study materials. And finally they must deal with a host of age-old complaints.

"On the one hand," declared Craig T. Senft, president of Silver Burdett, a major schoolbook publisher, "come the scholars and intellectuals, who complain that textbooks are badly written, so bland as to be inconclusive, so pedantically conceived that they insult the capabilities of children. On the other hand, come the minority groups—everyone from the D.A.R. to the Texans for America—with their own set of complaints. It's subversive to mention the United Nations, or to include Carl Sandburg in an English anthology. Or the B'nai B'rith complains if a phrase appears stating, 'and then Christ was turned over to the Jewish mob.' Other groups object just as strenuously if you take it out."

Faced with so many complex problems, some old, but most of them new, the textbook industry finds itself in deeper ferment than it has ever been during its two-hundred-year-old history.

We can begin to describe some of the dilemmas and challenges facing the industry by offering a case history of how Harper & Row, one of the nation's leading publishers, created a series of best-selling elementary-school textbooks. Entitled *Today's Basic Science*, the Harper & Row series consists of seven teacher's manuals plus seven different textbooks which teach general science to children from kindergarten through the sixth grade. Published in 1963, this series is the basic source of nearly all the science over one million grade-school children are now learning.

CHAPTER *2*

"Look, Ma, No Sperm Cells"

PROFESSOR JOHN GABRIEL NAVARRA sat in his office in Grossnickle Hall, fittingly named after Foster Grossnickle, the retired author of a best-selling elementary math series, and reflected on what textbook publishing had wrought. The son of a chemist, a Ph.D. from Columbia, a full professor and chairman of the science department at Jersey City State College at twenty-nine, Dr. Navarra is still possessed with a round boyish face and an enormous enthusiasm for his work. As the co-author of *Today's Basic Science*, Professor Navarra has so far received over $50,000 in royalties. Within the next ten years, his publisher will probably pay him an additional half a million dollars.

"Sure, I'm interested in good sales," he said, "just because money is a way of keeping score. But I don't think money has changed me. I like a little office. Plain steel bookcase and desk. Nothing plush. The president and dean have that. Why, I still wear open-collar shirts even though the president has a prohibition against it."

For all the accolades he has received, none, he feels, equals the fact that he has become the senior author of a series of children's textbooks. "Why does Johnson want to be President?" he asked. "Because it is the height of his profession. I wanted to write books for children and be the senior author. The senior author has the final say in the books and the program. Yes, I enjoy it. I like the flow of words, to see things in print. It has a lasting quality about it. Quite frankly I do not know of anything I'd like to do more."

Then his voice became confidential. "You know," he said, "I'd work for free. But I am not going to tell *them*."

Bob Hay is one of *them*. He is the editor in charge of *Today's Basic Science* and the science director of the textbook division of Harper & Row, located in Evanston, Illinois, a college town and Chicago suburb. A former newspaperman and once the science editor for an encyclopedia, Hay now spends his working days in a book-lined cubicle about half the size of Professor Navarra's office. Hay himself is an anomaly in the textbook industry; he has never taken a course in education and has never taught a class of students. "I've picked up some of the teacher's jargon," he said, "but I still don't feel at home at some of those educational meetings."

It is Bob Hay's opinion that one of the reasons textbooks are so dull to read is that they are written by teacher-authors and then rewritten by ex-teacher editors. "The stodginess of textbooks," he declared, "simply reflects the lack of imagination on the part of teachers."

Although Hay's name does not appear anywhere in the series' seven texts and seven teacher's guides, he probably had as much to do with the books' success as their two authors. For his contribution, which was substantial, Hay receives a yearly salary of somewhat more than $12,000, compared to the $100,000 in anticipated annual royalties which will be equally shared by the two men whose names appear on the books. In keeping with the practice of the textbook industry, Hay's reward consists of the encomium of his colleagues and the praise of his employer.

The plan to bring forth a new textbook series did not originate with Hay but with two of his superiors, Gordon Jones, then president, and Walter Brackman, at the time editor-in-chief of Row, Peterson, a Midwest textbook house that later merged with Harper, a famous trade-book publisher. In 1956, a year before Sputnik and seven years before the first books in the series were published, Jones and Brackman concluded that the more than eighty different science pamphlets Row had been selling would never capture a large enough chunk of the school market. Though they covered almost every science topic from insects to astronomy, these pamphlets contained only thirty pages each and had softcover bindings. Schools, however, prefer texts bound with hard covers on the theory that hardcover books can be reread many times and are thus less costly than paperbacks which tend to fall apart after six months' use.

"We sold millions of these pamphlets to the elementary schools," Jones said. "But they were always used as supplements to the basic science courses. We realized that what the teachers wanted were hardbound textbooks which organized the courses for them."

To find out whether the schools would purchase a thirteenth hardbound elementary science series (there were already a dozen on the market), the publisher mailed questionnaires to two thousand elementary-school teachers and assigned its eighty salesmen to interview dozens more. The firm sought to learn what the teachers wanted in a basic textbook and what they liked and disliked in the different series put out by Row's competitors.

The sharpest criticism leveled by the teachers was that many of the then current textbooks were little more than Dick and Jane type readers with a smattering of science.

And the science that appeared in even the better books turned out to be repetitive. For example, in the first grade all a child learned about electricity and magnetism was that a magnet picked up some objects but not others. In the second grade he identified the objects the magnet attracted as made of metal. In the third grade he discovered that a coil wrapped around a dry cell turned into a magnet. Finally, in the fourth grade he made the switch to electricity, lighting a light bulb with an electric circuit. What the teachers wanted was a grade-school textbook series that taught electricity, meteorology, astronomy, and atomic energy in depth to children at earlier ages. They also wanted more experiments youngsters could do in the classroom and something about how scientists thought and worked. The only major science series that fulfilled much of what the teachers sought had been published by D. C. Heath in 1953. "There was," said Jones, "a real opening in the market."

The next crucial step was to find a science editor capable of overseeing the series. Brackman first offered the job to Joseph Zafforoni, then an associate professor of education at the University of Nebraska. Though Zafforoni declined the offer, he agreed to co-author with John Navarra a book for teachers on how science should be taught in the elementary schools.

In the meantime Hay had been hired as an editor and his first task was the Navarra-Zafforoni book for science teachers. Late one afternoon in the spring of 1959, Bob Hay was at work in his Evanston office when he was confronted by the imposing figure of Gordon Jones.

"Do you think we would be making a mistake if we were to put together a hardbound science series?" Jones asked.

It was the first intimation that Hay had that Row was considering such a project. "I was aware," he recalled much later, "that they had been pushing this paperback series as a basal text. I was new on the staff, had only been here about eighteen months. I felt that if I should initiate the recommendation that they put out a hardbound text, they might think I was telling them what they had been doing for the past twenty years was all wrong."

Though Hay had played no part in the market research, he readily agreed that Row should undertake the publication of a standard hardbound elementary science series.

Jones then asked, "Do you think these people you are working with now, Navarra and Zafforoni, could turn out a series?"

From a professional standpoint, Hay thought, Zafforoni and Navarra were eminently qualified. They were recognized by school people across the country as specialists in science education, because of the speeches they made and the papers they wrote. Zafforoni had just completed a term as president of the Council for Elementary Science, International, and Navarra had then succeeded him.

In answer to Gordon Jones's question, Hay simply replied, "Yes, they can do the series."

Bob Hay now recalls that day with awe. "Ye gods," he said, "I lose sleep just thinking how casually Gordon Jones walked into my office and committed the company to spending a half-million dollars."

Actually Jones's decision was not quite that casual. Nor did Navarra and Zafforoni take their assignment lightly. Navarra, for instance, says he had already had the idea for a new grade-school science series in 1955 and began working on a first draft a year before Jones and Brackman made their initial decision to produce hardbound science textbooks. By 1959 the authors were working eighty hours a week and began submitting the manuscripts for the first four grades in 1960 and 1961. In September of 1961 Row put the books on a definite production schedule which would culminate in a

1963 publication date. Also starting in the fall of 1961, Hay started working ten hours a day, six to seven days a week, a brutal pace that would continue without letup for two years.

"The first thing I had to do," Hay said, "was establish a rapport with the authors so they would have confidence in me. It was the authors' function to contribute the basic ideas and philosophy of the program, which they did."

Next Hay handed the authors a detailed critique of the first draft of four books in the series. "Then," he said, "I moved in and rewrote pretty extensively. This is typical in textbook publishing. The rewrite involved English, organization, and content. Sometimes certain concept areas do not show up in the manuscript which should be there if you are to have a well-rounded textbook. For instance, the authors had just barely outlined photosynthesis for the fifth grade. What I did was a wholesale rewrite."

One of Hay's first major problems was to fit the authors' ideas into the limited vocabularies demanded by the elementary-school teachers, who insist that the average grade-school child can cope only with the simplest words. Hay's problem was compounded by the fact that he was trying to produce interesting textbooks on science and scientific words do not appear on the vocabulary lists made up by the reading experts.

Hay began checking the original draft of the first-grade book against the Spache readability formula which uses sentence length and a list of 769 words to measure readability. Hay soon discovered that according to the formula the first-grade text was pitched to the reading ability of the average child in the fourth month of the second grade. "It was a shattering experience," he recalled. "I knew the sales department would be horrified."

The editor discussed the problem with the authors. "We agreed," he said, "that it would be sheer folly to water down science in order to control vocabulary." Hay then worked out a compromise. He did not count the scientific vocabulary when he checked the words against the Spache list. At the same time Hay substituted or deleted words in the non-science vocabulary which hopefully would make the book easier to read and thus acceptable to the schools. A typical passage Hay changed was this section about airplanes in the first-grade text. Originally the authors had written:

Airplanes come and go.
They take off from an airport.
They fly through the air.
They land at the airport.

In the published version, the "Airplanes come and go. They fly *in* the air." But they never land. Hay had to eliminate the words "airport" and "land" and change "through" to "in" because they did not appear on the word list he was using. For the same reason Hay changed the phrase "bubbles, bubbles everywhere" to "bubbles, bubbles all around," because "everywhere" is not on the vocabulary list. However, the word "bubbles" continued to float through the text even though the reading experts felt it was too difficult for young children to learn.

"You just can't eliminate 'bubbles,'" Bob Hay declared, "because the reading people have decided bubbles is a subject you should not write about. I am also sure that a word like 'airport' is easy for a six-year-old to learn. But if I had kept in these and other words it might have made the difference between success and failure of the entire series."

"It's inevitable," he added, "that vocabulary lists control content."

They also tend to infuse textbook prose with a stilted, singsong quality. The authors and editors, for instance, must not only consider word difficulty but sentence length, making both fit into the readability formulas. Here, for example, is what a nine-year-old child reads as he begins the study of rocks and earth in the fourth-grade text of *Today's Basic Science*:

"Go to the beach. There is sand on the beach. There are rocks, too. There are many rocks on the sandy beach.

"Most of the rocks are small. They are pebbles. But others are large . . . Rocks are everywhere."

"The editor's problem," Bob Hay continued, "is not to get it choppy. And boy, this is difficult. I don't think we succeeded in the fourth grade."

Another problem that distressed Hay concerned the number of new words that could be introduced on a page. It is the general rule that no more than two words which are not on the vocabulary list can appear on a page of text. "This horrifies me," Hay said. Hay decided to apply the Dale-Chall formula to the fourth- through sixth-grade texts. However, the editor and the authors not only introduced a number of common English words which the Dale-Chall list refuses to recognize, but they peppered the text with numerous scientific or technical terms.

"For example, in the fourth-grade book," Hay explained, "we boldly teach three main kinds of rocks—sedimentary, igneous, and metamorphic. I can assure you those three words are not on the vocabulary list for the fourth grader. Certainly the words and the concepts taught about these rocks are not beyond him.

"I would like to think," he said, "that our science series represents a breakthrough. There were times, though, when management wondered if I wasn't up to something that would bankrupt the organization."

While his superiors permitted Hay to crack the taboo against words like "bubbles" and "igneous," he was simply forbidden to mention Darwin's theory of evolution. "The president of the company only put one query to me," he recalled. " 'Are you saying anything about evolution in these books?' I had already concluded that we are not saying anything about evolution. Because of the opposition of Protestant fundamentalists, our series does not mention it. In fact, no reference is made to evolution in any elementary-school science series."

Later when the books came up for submission to school authorities in Tennessee, a state then endowed with the memory of the Scopes Trial, the firm's Tennessee salesman carefully checked the textbooks for even an oblique reference to the author of the theory of natural selection. Upon reading page 108 of the book for sixth graders, the salesman became alarmed.

"Scientists," the passage told him, "believe these simple multicelled animals came about through the union of one-celled animals. Gradually, one-celled animals grouped together and formed many-celled animals. Scientists have set forth many explanations and reasons for this occurrence. No one is really sure."

Although the passage puts the textbook publisher in that enviable commercial position which permits him to offend no one, the firm's Tennessee salesman took a different point of view, suggesting to Hay that indeed the text, if it did not mention Darwin, at least bordered on evolution. Hay in turn reassured him that "we had not introduced a discussion of evolution or defined it as such. We were only talking about the lower forms of life and had not cast any aspersions on the dignity of man. In fact, the authors themselves had not included the theory of evolution in their draft of the text because they felt it was not necessary."

Assuaged and armed, the salesman had no trouble convincing the Tennessee authorities to adopt the books.

While the textbook publisher managed to ignore Darwin and his theory, he could not deny the existence of an even more fundamental subject, sex. "By the time youngsters get into the sixth grade," Bob Hay explained, "their hormones begin stirring around a little. They become aware of their own sexual interest. To a younger child in the fifth grade, you can teach human reproduction in a detached way. The older youngsters who are aware of sex and who know more are inclined to snicker in the classroom. This was the one content area where I asked for personal advice."

Actually both Hay and the authors wanted to introduce an explanation of reproduction in the sixth-grade book. Besides hoping to satisfy the typical eleven-year-old's curiosity, the authors and their editor felt the educator's compulsion to explain the source of life to the nation's schoolchildren. If they succeeded, Harper & Row would become the first textbook publisher of a basic science textbook that fully explained *human* reproduction to elementary-school pupils. To achieve this breakthrough, the authors wrote the following passage:

The Very Beginning of Development
(Illustration—Pix 1—Show magnified diagram of an egg-cell.
Label parts—nucleus, protoplasm.
Pix 2—Sperm-cell with parts labeled—head, centerpiece, tail)

Animal life begins when two cells unite. These two cells are the raw materials in order for living things to reproduce. One of these cells is called an egg-cell. This is the female cell. The other cell is the sperm-cell. It is the male cell. The union of these two cells is known as fertilization. It is at this moment of union that life begins. Each of these two cells performs a special task in order for development to occur.

This introductory passage was followed by a detailed, but equally bland, description of the egg and sperm cells and how they function. Next came a section on human reproduction, which was just as bland and factual. It contained the following description:

> In many ways your growth and development were very similar to that of the other animals that you have just read about.
> You, too, began life as a fertilized cell. This fertilized cell was started and grew in a special organ in your mother's body. This organ is called the uterus. Once the egg-cell was fertilized by the sperm-cell, it grew and divided again and again into trillions of cells. [The passage then goes on to explain such concepts and terms as blastula, placenta, umbilical cord, and the development of the human embryo.]

While Hay himself felt some schools might object to an explanation of *human* reproduction, he and the authors hoped that a description of *animal* reproduction would prove acceptable to the teachers who would select the books and the communities which would pay for them. Interestingly, not at issue was the emotional maturity of eleven-year-olds to deal with the subject or their intellectual capacity to understand it. On September 7, 1962, Hay circulated a memorandum to his superiors and it is quoted in full for it provides its own commentary on how a textbook publisher decides what material he should include in a textbook. Editor Hay wrote:

> Book 6 of TODAY'S BASIC SCIENCE includes a unit on the growth and development of animals. The unit puts forth a rather detailed explanation of animal reproduction. It defines both *sexual* (sperm and egg cell) and *asexual* (simple cell division) procreation among protozoa and the higher animals.
> We recommend that the unit be published. It is typical of the authors' desire to upgrade science instruction in the elementary

grades. Moreover, it represents the thinking that is now going on among the professors (see *Embryology*, a science unit compiled by the Elementary School Science Project, University of California). We are in line with the trends.

The unit is straightforward, factual, and scientific. It contains nothing that should be offensive to parents or teachers. (We deleted a section on human reproduction from the authors' manuscript.) Yet, in view of the subject, we feel that it possibly borders on a sales problem. Therefore, we recommend that it be checked out by the sales department and by those who have had experience in sales.

Other elementary series are less mature in their presentation of this subject. Singer goes into the same details in its Book 8. (For 8th graders) American Book Company describes reproduction fully in Book 7. (For 7th graders) Heath says politely that birds and frogs come out of eggs. Mammals never come to birth in a Heath book. They just happen to be around to get milk from their mothers.

This material of course appears in high-school biology texts. It is not new to the classroom. Grade placement is the problem we are considering—not the subject as such.

Hay then took the passage describing *animal* reproduction and showed it to an elementary-school principal in Evanston, a science teacher in Wilmette, Illinois, the firm's seven regional managers, and the Florida salesman who would be responsible for obtaining the first major state adoption of the series.

"While the principal and the teacher okayed inclusion of the sperm and egg cells," Hay recalled, "the salesmen said we had gone a little too far to be safe. I got a little nervous and queasy. Suppose people in Florida look on the subject gingerly and for this reason alone your books are eliminated. Then you have made a mistake. The conclusion was to soft-pedal all the details of animal reproduction."

Hay then boiled down the passages quoted earlier to this single paragraph:

> Almost all mammals bring forth living young. The offspring develops inside the female's body. The growing organism receives food and oxygen from the mother. A system of blood vessels carries this nourishment to the embryo.

In effect what Bob Hay had done was to eliminate all references to human reproduction and then dilute the description of animal reproduction by removing any mention of terms and concepts like the egg cell and fertilization. As Hay himself put it, "We now teach reproduction without ever introducing the sperm cell."

In his office at Jersey City State College, Professor John Navarra, the senior author, explained that the omission was an act of "educational statesmanship." "The final decision of what goes into the schools rests with the lay boards of education," he said. "The schools do belong to the people and the schools are an extension of the home and community. It is not our job to introduce something that subverts the community.

"It would have been distinctive to have included reproduction," he went on. "But the important thing is to move the educational program forward and not start brush fires. As strongly as I feel about teaching the concepts of reproduction, you can be ahead of your time."

Back in Evanston, Bob Hay was haunted by the dilemma of the sixth-grade teacher using a textbook which still presented the reproductive process as a miraculous act. "What does the teacher do," he mused, "when a kid asks, 'But how *did* the offspring develop inside the female body?' Nowhere in this textbook do we explain the process." *

---

* Reproduction is finally given a scientific explanation when the series reaches the junior-high-school level.

A more subtle but equally basic issue deeply concerned Frederick Seyfarth, the firm's art director. Since 1936, when Row discarded the traditional black-and-white pictures, schoolbooks have been turned into pyres of color photography and drawings. Consequently, much of the artwork a child sees today consists of illustrations used in schoolbooks. Thus the art directors of the textbook houses play an important role in the development of the artistic tastes of the nation's students.

Working with 40 free-lance artists, Seyfarth commissioned and planned over 2,500 illustrations, at least one for every page of every textbook which made up *Today's Basic Science*. Some of the artists, Seyfarth explained, work full time illustrating schoolbooks. They draw as many as five different illustrations a week and earn as much as $40,000 annually. The average price comes to around $100 per picture but rises to about $300 for an illustration as complicated as a painting depicting a symphony orchestra. "One of our best illustrators," he said, "learned art through correspondence school and makes about thirty thousand dollars a year.

"What I try to do," the art director added, "is to get the best artists working for us. Some artists can draw people, but they do not render what we want. In a science book it does not matter if people have personalities. People are incidental props. In a reader you have social situations. That's where the artist makes people human and tells the story in human terms."

Seyfarth first selected and then assigned the precise topic he wanted illustrated. For instance, the artist who specialized in animals was told to bring in a preliminary drawing, which Seyfarth had to approve. The artist then returned with a completed drawing. All the illustrations had to be in four colors, which gave the texts a rich magazine appearance, but which also added about 25 percent to the cost of publishing the books, an expense then passed on to the schools that bought them.

"We are selling these books to school superintendents, teachers, and state-board committees and these people prefer color," Seyfarth said. "They believe color motivates the student. But there is no valid scientific study I can point to that proves this. In my opinion it is certainly possible to do a complete teaching job with little color. However, the chance of selling the books is reduced.

"But gingerbread as such is not my big problem. What I worry about concerns levels of taste. And here I have to walk a tightrope. We are trying to please a mass market and at the same time do something that is forward looking and stimulating. We are so accustomed to seeing three grinning boys and a girl playing with a magnet. Yet if children see nothing but this kind of trite, ordinary art, they will never appreciate anything better."

Much of the artwork Seyfarth commissioned had to be literal and realistic since its main purpose was to illustrate scientific experiments and topics like the atom and the human nervous system. But the art director also included several impressionistic paintings such as a picture of a cyclone striking an island and another showing a quiet night scene in a city. "If all the art represented this kind of art," Seyfarth said, "the dear little old ladies on the textbook selection committee and the salesmen would be horrified. Our problem is that we can make better books than we can sell."

Toward the end of 1962 and the beginning of 1963, *Today's Basic Science* began rolling off the presses, and with the appearance of the freshly printed copies loomed the most nervewracking question of all: Would the series sell? Navarra and Zafforoni had already spent eight years developing, testing, and writing the texts. Over one million words

had passed through Bob Hay's hand. The production department had expended $100,000 just to produce the hand-
drawn, four-color illustrations. Advertising was preparing to
spend $92,000 in educational journals and brochures, and
sales was in the process of giving away 100,000 copies to
teachers who indicated they might be interested in using
the books. In brief, the textbook publisher had already
spent $525,000 and had yet to sell a single book.

The first major sales test came in February, 1963, in
Florida. Seven years had passed since that state had adopted
a new elementary science series and as a result competition
promised to be stiff. Eight publishers had submitted as many
different series for consideration by a statewide textbook
selection committee consisting mostly of classroom teachers.
However, under the law, the committee could recommend
only three different series which the Florida State Board of
Education then had to approve. The committee's and the
Board's decisions would prove crucial since local schools
could only use those textbooks which the two groups
sanctioned. In sum, if Florida selected the Harper & Row
series, it would not only mean a probable sale of 200,000
books but would also indicate that the publisher had guessed
right, that other schools in other states would want to adopt
a series with a more difficult depth-approach to science.

The fate of *Today's Basic Science* rested with Tom Shannon, the firm's Florida salesman. For the previous eight years
Shannon had been cultivating the state's teachers and he
was prepared now to make the supreme selling effort. Ten
months before the Board of Education met to decide which
books the state would adopt, Shannon and another salesman
began a thousand-mile journey that took them from Pensa-
cola to Key West. Along the way they visited six thousand
teachers, supervisors, and principals, met with sixty-seven
county textbook committees, and had interviews with the

twelve members of the all-powerful state selection committee. To all Shannon showed either the galleys or the published books. He sought the reaction and comments of the state's teachers and in turn hoped that county committees would recommend the Harper & Row series to the state committee. It was largely on Shannon's recommendation that the chapter on reproduction had been watered down. "I talked to a dozen or so teachers and supervisors," he said, "and it seemed putting the topic at the sixth-grade level just might prove too sensational."

Finally, at 2 P.M., on February 26, 1963, the Florida salesmen, the firm's general sales manager, Harvey Hanlon, and several dozen other bookmen filed into the ornate State Senate Chamber in Tallahassee. As the Harper & Row salesmen took their seats, they were handed a twenty-seven-page booklet listing all the choices of the various grade- and high-school textbook committees, which had met in secret during the previous week. The salesmen nervously thumbed through the booklet and just two pages from the end they found the recommendations for elementary science. At the top of the list were the Harper & Row books.

It was now up to Harvey Hanlon, the firm's head sales executive, to leap the last hurdle. Under the Florida system, each publisher whose book has been recommended by a state selection committee must submit a sealed bid guaranteeing the prices he will charge for five years, the standard period of most adoptions. Hanlon knew that if he offered to charge 10 percent more than the sum asked by his competitors, the Florida State Board of Education might reject the series even though the committee had recommended it. And rejection, Hanlon realized, could easily mean a loss in sales of at least $200,000.

Hanlon, his palms slighly moist, wrote out the Harper & Row prices, placed them in a sealed envelope, and then joined the other bookmen outside the Senate Chamber. For the next hour the salesmen anxiously paced up and down the hallway while the Board and the elementary-textbook selection committee met in executive session.

At last the large oaken doors swung open and the bookmen once again took up their seats. A hush settled over the huge room. This time no one looked at the dull, aging portraits of Florida's former Senate presidents that festooned the walls. Instead, the salesmen turned toward Thomas Bailey, state superintendent of schools, who arose to announce the textbooks Florida would adopt for the next five years. Again Harper & Row had won. "I can only tell you I was relieved that it was over," said Tom Shannon. "The risks and gamble are tremendous. You spend all that time and it could all come to nothing."

About the moment Harvey Hanlon and Tom Shannon were celebrating with bourbon and water in a Tallahassee hotel room, the firm's president strolled into Hay's office in Evanston. Earlier that day Arizona, a state adoption system with fewer schools, had selected the series, and now Florida, the big one, had come through. "Well, Bob," he said, grinning broadly, "we made it."

"It was a unique experience," Bob Hay recalled. "We're a conservative lot. We are not given to martini lunches and it is simply not assumed that the president of the company, two editors, and the art director would be bending elbows together. But on that day we were."

As the year proceeded it seemed that *Today's Basic Science* could not be stopped. Over a half-dozen states, mostly in the South, had sought new science textbooks, and the schoolbooks they invariably selected included those published by Harper & Row. In addition, cities like New York, Philadelphia, Boston, Cincinnati, and Omaha either listed or adopted the new series.

"All this adds up to a remarkable achievement in sales—a successful selling job," Hay said, in a private memorandum which he sent to the sales force. "We suspect," he went on, "that in each instance the agent hurdles many obstacles that at first appeared insurmountable. For, as anyone who knows the subject can attest, the competition in science is formidable. It's *rough*. There are other good books around . . . good books bearing the imprint *not* of Harper & Row but of Heath, Singer, Macmillan, Scott, Foresman, and American Book."

As is the typical practice of the industry, Hay also ripped into the competing texts, giving the Harper & Row salesmen a varied assortment of verbal buckshot with which they could blast the series issued by the other publishers. His strongest comments were reserved for the Heath science series, the most successful of all the elementary science texts on the market. Heath understandably had the most to lose in a sales battle with an upstart challenger, and according to the Harper & Row salesmen, the Heath bookmen were doing their best to shoot down the Navarra and Zafforoni texts.

In a separate memorandum devoted just to an attack on the Heath series, Hay told his own bookmen the Heath editors had supplied the Heath salesmen with a "hair-splitting critique" of *Today's Basic Science*.

"Obviously," Hay wrote, "the Heath people are employing these tactics because they find it difficult to deal with our basic program. They are desperate, frustrated, and frightened. . . . If necessary, we can respond in kind to Heath's attacks. The Heath science series is an excellent set of books (a fact we cannot deny; or can we?). But, in spite of their wide use and numerous revisions, the Heath science texts do reflect major weaknesses."

While praising the Heath books as being unexcelled in the experiments they asked young children to perform ("John

Navarra and Joe Zafforoni," Hay wrote, "have said that Heath moved into its eminent position through its use of the one word 'experiment,'"), Hay proceeded to demolish almost everything else in the Heath series. In a section-by-section and at times page-by-page analysis of the grade-six Heath book, *Science for Today and Tomorrow*, Hay titillated his own salesmen with comments like:

Page 102. Heath has challenged our picture of the mercury barometer in *Book 4*. According to our information, the Heath men are saying that we have suggested the use of 40 pounds of mercury costing more than a school could possibly afford. The criticism is neither valid nor threatening. But, if we choose to respond in kind, we might call attention to the flask of mercury pictured on this page in the Heath sixth-grade text. Doesn't this picture suggest that classroom quantities of mercury are rather large? (Actually, the supply houses package mercury in pill-sized bottles.) All this, of course, is petty and irrelevant in judging the merits of a textbook.

Page 336, last paragraph: "Each radium atom has one flash of atomic energy in it, and that's all." Is this a science text or a science-fiction paperback? The statement is ludicrous. In reality, a single atom of any element packs quite a wallop upon being split. Nuclear energy can hardly be looked upon as a mere flash. Could it be that Heath's authors and editors have never come across Einstein's famous equation: $E = mc^2$?

Pages 363–364. These pages are blank, like many others in Heath's little story-book. Such is the quality of a warmed-over, nine-year-old textbook that missed the mark in the first place.

As Hay himself readily admitted later, these critiques aimed at downgrading the competition were just part of the textbook selling game. "I don't deny," he said, "that my critique is opinionated. I have books to sell and so do our competitors. I have to indoctrinate our salesmen, help them see the strong points of our books and the weak points of those put out by our competitors."

Then in December, 1963, just one month after Hay had circulated his Heath memorandum, a financial bombshell exploded in Harper & Row's Evanston offices. The Newark Textbook Council, which selects books for New Jersey's largest public school system, rejected the series even though it thought the books were the best grade-school science texts on the market. In a brief letter the Council accused the publisher of using "stereotyped middle class" illustrations. The Newark Council also charged that the publisher had failed to include any pictures or text "relating to minority groups." What the Council really meant was that not one illustration in the entire series showed a Negro child, teacher, or scientist.

Shortly after receiving the letter from Newark, Hay fired off still another memorandum, this one to the firm's president and to the editor-in-chief. Hay readily admitted that "we made no self-conscious effort to 'integrate' the science textbooks," but he denied that the textbooks showed only stereotyped, middle-class people.

He pointed to a first-grade illustration depicting a child wearing a tee shirt. "Can anyone say," Hay wrote, "whether he is a child destined for enrollment in an Ivy League college or in a subway school within a big city? Our feeling is that he is neither middle class nor underprivileged. He is merely the boy next door, whatever his economic status. This is the picture we deliberately attempted."

Finally, he noted the drawing of the human brain in the sixth-grade text. "The tones," he declared, "were deliberately selected to suggest the brain of *homo sapiens*—not specifically the brain of a white man, a black man, a red man, a yellow man, or a brown man. This, we feel, is truly an example of scientific objectivity."

The top executives of the company knew that Hay's memo would not satisfy the Newark Council, or the demands that would be forthcoming from cities like Detroit which had in effect called for textbooks with integrated illustrations a year earlier. To meet the requirements of the urban school market, the company decided to publish an "Intercultural Edition." The text would be exactly the same as the all-white edition, but about one-third of the illustrations would portray Negroes, with a sprinkling of Orientals and Mexicans. All would be shown in poses identical to those held by the whites.

Hay and the art director's next problem was to decide how the Negroes should look. "We had always been criticized for showing only handsome, suburban white children," Hay said. "Should we take the same approach with the Negroes? Should we show straight hair or be more authentic and show kinky hair? Upon my recommendation, we instructed our artists that in all instances Negro women had to be attractive and fashionable. I followed one other rule. Under no circumstances were colored people to be shown in a menial activity. In our integrated text in grade two we show a piano mover and a truck loader. Both are white. Our sincere objective was to meet the most remote interests of the integrationists."

Within the year Harper & Row had published a separate "integrated" science series and Newark said it was delighted. But in Peoria, Illinois, new objections were raised by integrationists who complained that no Negro appeared in an illustration of a symphony orchestra. As it turned out, it was the only large group scene the firm had failed to integrate. The Peoria critics also found fault with a picture depicting a Negro father and his little girl standing on a wooden porch gazing up at the moon and stars. According to those who objected to the illustration, the wooden porch reflected a lower-class background and thus was biased against Negroes. Peoria solved the problem by adopting the non-integrated edition which showed a white father and his little girl perched on the identical wooden porch. At the same time, several school districts in Georgia turned down the "Inter-cultural Edition" because of two illustrations, the first show-ing a white and a Negro boy sitting together on a large grandfather's chair, the second depicting a group of Negro and white children swimming in the same pool.

"Try as we will," said Bob Hay, "we will be criticized."

CHAPTER *3*

Authors, Editors, and the Prince of Denmark

THE TEXTBOOK INDUSTRY and the product it produces form a series of curious ironies: though teachers often clamor for books that are different and stimulating, they usually turn down the schoolbook that is daringly different; though textbooks are used as the basis of lectures and class discussions, the ex-teacher editors who produce them rarely if ever visit a classroom; though teachers and curriculum experts insist that one of the most important things a child can do is to acquire a passion for reading, the schoolbooks he is invariably given contain the least inspiring prose; though publishers tell students that in America everyone has the right to express his ideas freely, the schoolbook publisher frequently is the first to bow to censorship; though the industry is one of the smallest in the country—we spend more on dog food than we do on schoolbooks—it may well have greater influence on shaping the thoughts and values of the nation than all the mass media combined. To delve into these ironies and to explain them will be the aim of this chapter and those that follow.

Although textbook publishers may be considered creators of a mass market product—over 151 million grade- and high-school textbooks were purchased in 1966—the industry itself remains only a multimillion-dollar midget among the multi-billion-dollar giants like steel and cars. In fact, despite the important role textbooks play in education, schools spend 1½ to 2 percent of their total budget on books. This can be explained by the fact that textbooks are relatively inexpensive (in 1966 the average cost of a hardbound book for a grade-school child came to $2.26, for a high-school student, $3.42). Moreover, most of the school budget goes to fixed costs like teachers' salaries which cannot be cut. Schoolbooks, on the other hand, frequently make up the last item in the budget and the one that is easiest to pare.

Yet, as small as it is in comparison to other mass producers, the textbook industry is in the process of becoming a very big business indeed, particularly when one compares it to private entrepreneurs like that twentieth-century throwback to Adam Smith, the trade-book publisher. Certainly no financier or growth-stock gambler need look askance at schoolbook publishers who in 1966 sold $420 million worth of elementary- and high-school textbooks.* Like so many other portents of affluence in America this figure was conceived during the baby boom that followed World War II and is statistically represented by more than a 700 percent increase in annual schoolbook sales over 1945.

As so often happens when an industry becomes highly successful, individual companies begin to lose their corporate identity. In fact, during the past decade, few industries in America have been so consumed by the twin fevers of merger and acquisition as textbook publishing. Thus in 1958 there were more than sixty-two elementary- and high-school

---

* Of this sum approximately $15 million came from the federal government under the Elementary and Secondary Education Act.

houses. Today there are fifty-six. At one time many of these firms specialized in grade or secondary texts and thus went after only one part of the school market. But as the market expanded, they sought an inexpensive device for their own quick growth so that they could meet the soaring demand for schoolbooks. The solution was merger and the results were publishing giants like Harcourt, Brace & World, and Holt, Rinehart and Winston, which now embrace the entire school market from kindergarten through college.

But this was only the beginning. What may turn out to be the wave of the future was the entry of the huge electronic firms like I.B.M., Xerox, General Electric, and R.C.A. into educational publishing. In 1963, I.B.M. made its first acquisition in thirty years when it purchased Science Research Associates, a Chicago-based education publisher, for $62 million worth of I.B.M. stock. Others that followed were: Xerox, which bought American Education Publications, a publisher of weekly newspapers and math and science journals for 16,500,000 schoolchildren, and General Electric, which joined forces with Time, Inc., to form General Learning Corporation, a $37,500,000 publisher of educational materials. Tossed into that marriage were Silver Burdett, a textbook subsidiary of Time, Inc., and the brains of a thousand General Electric Ph.D.'s. All these mergers and acquisitions were followed in 1966 by Raytheon's purchase of D. C. Heath and R.C.A.'s ingestion of Random House. In 1967, C.B.S. and Holt, Rinehart and Winston announced their merger.

"Companies like I.B.M., Xerox, and General Electric know there is a big, growing, safe market in education," declared Theodore Sizer, the thirty-three-year-old dean of Harvard's Graduate School of Education. "These companies bought the educational houses to find out what they did. The real big change will come when they decide what to do."

In the meantime the traditional publisher will continue

to produce the textbooks that will teach your child much of what he will learn in school.

To discover how textbook publishers operate one must travel to three cities: New York, Boston, and Chicago. Over a century ago these communities formed the great population centers of the country, and it was for that reason they became the headquarters for nearly all the grade- and high-school publishers, including the dozen or so major firms that currently account for over 60 percent of the schoolbooks sold. Among the leaders there are now four giants in the field: Scott, Foresman in suburban Chicago, and Ginn in Boston, the two biggest elementary publishers, and in New York, Harcourt, Brace & World, and Holt, Rinehart and Winston, the two largest secondary-school publishers. These firms are followed in New York and New Jersey by McGraw-Hill, Prentice-Hall, Crowell-Collier and Macmillan, Silver Burdett, and American Book Company. In Chicago there is Follet and in nearby Evanston, Illinois, the textbook division of Harper & Row. And finally, there are the Boston firms of D. C. Heath, Allyn and Bacon, Houghton Mifflin, and Addison-Wesley, the outrider and fastest-growing company in the industry.

Almost all of these firms are fifty to a hundred years old. In contrast, Addison-Wesley, a small printing company and college publisher during World War II, did not enter school-book publishing until 1958. Four years later Addison-Wesley brought forth its first-grade school series, a collection of math books which use color and graphic designs to show how math works. This visual approach proved so popular that the Addison-Wesley series accounted for about half the elementary math sales in the country in 1965, an incredible accomplishment since it usually takes at least a decade or longer for a textbook publisher to establish his name, editorial and sales know-how. Largely as a result of the math series' success, Addison-Wesley's sales rocketed from $8,300,000 in 1964 to nearly $16,000,000 in 1965, and the firm is now preparing to take on the entire school market, something which no company has done from a dead start for over a quarter of a century. As a way of urging its employees to reach even greater heights, the company recently posted a brief note on the cafeteria bulletin board. The notice said that if anyone had bothered to buy a single share of Addison-Wesley stock for $200 in 1947 it would be worth $80,000.

"I don't think we are any smarter than say Scott, Foresman," declared Donald Jones, the forty-one-year-old executive vice-president of Addison-Wesley. "It's just that many of the old-line publishers are reluctant to move. They have sold something well for thirty years and they are afraid to let it go and start something new. Who knows? Maybe we'll be in that position some day."

More representative of the industry are houses like Scott, Foresman, and Ginn, which in 1966 together sold about $85 million worth of schoolbooks. Many of the texts these firms publish first appeared thirty years ago. In order to revise these books every five to ten years, the textbook houses maintain enormous editorial staffs. For its elementary reading series alone, Scott, Foresman has under contract twelve outside authors and consultants and in its employ seventy editors who edit the stories used in the books and who write the teacher's guides, the *Think and Do* workbooks, their manuals, and the standardized reading tests.

The reason for the employment of such huge editorial staffs is that the textbook publisher relies on a variety of specialists. For instance, a publisher like Scott, Foresman employs educators and editors who are expert in only one aspect of learning, such as phonics, or linguistics, or classroom pedagogy. In contrast, the trade-book publisher usually relies on only one author, one editor, and a single designer in the publication of each book. A basic difference between trade and schoolbook publishing was pointed up by Frank G. Jennings, the author of several textbook anthologies. In his essay, "Of Textbooks and Trapped Idealists," Jennings wrote:

> A book comes into being when some author, driven by his private daemon, brings forth a manuscript which some editor likes well enough to try to persuade a publisher to print. The book lives or dies by the size and loyalty of the readership it attracts. With textbooks it is otherwise. An editor, a publisher, a salesman, a successful teacher (or an unsuccessful one!), a curriculum specialist or a committee of many or all of these people may decide that a new textbook is needed or would succeed in a certain subject if it were done in a certain way.

Because, says Jennings, "a textbook is usually the product, not of a single man's midnight agony, but of a committee's mid-afternoon kaffee klatsch," it suffers from too many hands stirring too few pots. And as always must happen when the committee system of writing and editing prevails, the textbooks children study are totally lacking in individual style, private opinion, and personal passion. Understandably this observation is rarely volunteered by textbook publishers, though all are aware of it. An exception is William Jovanovich, the president of Harcourt, Brace & World, who once wrote, "It is curious that [textbook] publishers should continue to believe that committees can write well. None has, save the committee of scholars who in 1611 produced the King James Bible—and even here one suspects, knowing the way of committees, that some poor wretch was left with the work once the prayers were said and Bishop Lancelot Andrewes dismissed the meetings."

Like textbook editors and salesmen, most schoolbook authors have had a considerable amount of teaching experience. However, the few teachers who become textbook authors rarely possess even the rudimentary skills of the professional writer. In fact, as the person whose name appears on the cover, the teacher-author usually is the least consequential member of the textbook writing team. He hardly ever originates the idea for a textbook or series of schoolbooks. According to Sidney Gleason, the vice-president for administration at D. C. Heath, "A fraction of one percent of the ideas teachers send in over the transom ever come to fruition." (This again is in direct contrast to what happens in trade departments or houses where almost all the fiction and the viewpoint, if not the original theme, for non-fiction is the brainchild of the author. More important, of course, is that more often than not the name on the cover or jacket of a trade book is also the name of the author who wrote it, a phenomenon that rarely occurs in textbook publishing.)

Although the textbook author often contributes neither the original idea, a point of view, or the finished prose, he does offer the prestige of his title or position, which automatically supplies the endorsement of authority that most school selection committees seem to require. While most teachers and administrators would like to become textbook authors, few are chosen. (In contrast few college professors seek the assignment since writing a non-college text either is considered beneath their dignity or, more important, in the eyes of their colleagues fails to add to their academic status.) What usually happens is that the editors in the textbook houses seek out potential authors at conferences, in the schools, or through the education journals. Many authors are grade- or high-school teachers and others work as curriculum specialists, school administrators, education professors, and in a few instances as university scholars.

"Sometimes," explains Heath's Sidney Gleason, "we find them by going to the assistant superintendent of a school system like Shaker Heights or South Orange, New Jersey. It's our thesis that good salaries attract good people. We also look for people who are prominent in education, and we consider geographical origin. It does not do any harm if the author is a native of a big market state like Texas or California."

For many teachers, textbook authorship brings in a few thousand dollars a year. "Only two to five percent of the books hit the jackpot," Gleason said. "With most of the rest of the books you just get your bait back."

When the books do hit, however, the rewards are similar to owning an oil well. It is not unusual for each of the authors of a best-selling elementary- or high-school text to earn a half-million dollars over a ten-year period. A select few like Harper & Row's Mabel O'Donnell and Harcourt's John E. Warriner earn even more.

Harcourt, Brace & World began publishing Warriner's *English Grammar and Composition* series for grades 7 through 12 in 1948. Since then he has received over one million dollars in royalties. Though he was immensely successful, he continued to head a high-school English department on Long Island, New York, and only recently did he decide to build a house among a colony of millionaires in the Virgin Islands.

"One day he was invited to a party given by one of his very wealthy neighbors," recalled Cameron Moseley, an executive at Harcourt. "His host had asked him what he had done. 'I was an English teacher,' Warriner replied. Warriner waited until his neighbor recovered and then explained that he had written several books that had sold well. Said his host, 'You are the first teacher I have ever heard of who became a success.'"

The teams of teacher-authors usually owe most of their success to an anonymous team of ex-teacher editors whose entire working day is devoted to turning the authors' feckless prose into uninspired but readable English. The industry's opinion of its own teacher-authors was summed up by Grant Bennion, a former salesman who rose to become president of Ginn, a Boston publisher. "If you want to crucify somebody," he declared, "publish his book just as he wrote it. There is always room for a good editor."

Indeed there is, since he often supplies the pedagogy and the information plus the language which communicates both to the teacher or student. As previously noted, like the author, the textbook editor has had some teaching experience, a requirement insisted upon by publishers who believe this will make the editor familiar with the problems a teacher faces in the classroom. Also, since most elementary teachers are women, they usually fill the editorial jobs in the grade-school departments. In fact, more than any other industry textbook publishing has opened its doors to women with editorial ambitions. This becomes apparent at coffee-break time when the editorial offices of a typical elementary division take on the air of a smoky teachers' lounge.

Once a teacher becomes an editor, however, he or she almost never faces a class of students again. "Every September when I see all the kids going back to school, I regret that I gave up teaching," says Harley Mutzfeld, a forty-five-year-old math and science editor at D. C. Heath who spent eleven years on the faculty of Central Connecticut State College in New Britain. "Any good teacher finds real stimulation in seeing a live audience respond to his ideas. My thrill now is having a book I worked on presented to me. But how, I ask myself, is it going to work in the classroom? In publishing it may take months or years to know."

For many textbook editors there is the ultimate satisfaction in knowing that eventually they can influence the minds of hundreds of thousands of children instead of only thirty or forty youngsters in a classroom. However, the most compelling reason many teachers become textbook editors is out of sheer frustration with their teaching jobs. One young teacher joined D. C. Heath after spending two years in a schoolroom located on the second floor of a firehouse. She could no longer take the clanging bells and screaming sirens which went off under her classroom every time a house or store caught fire.

For Dr. Robert Page, who earned his doctorate at Yale, the frustrations grew more slowly. At forty-seven, Bob Page is still given to black knitted ties, tweed jackets, and musty pipes. For thirteen years he taught English in a Denver, Colorado, high school. Then came an offer to head the English department at Ginn, the Boston publisher for whom he had compiled and edited a short-story anthology in his spare time. If he accepted, it would mean giving up teaching, something he loved.

"It wasn't the youngsters," he explained. "They were good kids and there was plenty of funds for books." Nor was it primarily money, although Ginn offered him a starting salary of $11,500, $2,000 more than he was making as a teacher.

"I had just got a slow burn," he declared. "In the Midwest there is this tremendous emphasis on athletics and extra-curricular activities. Kids would come to me and say they hadn't done their homework because they had gone to a club meeting the previous night or they were pulled out of class for a school show. It had just reached the point where I didn't want to fight the school system any more."

Once word got out that he was leaving, a number of his fellow teachers came to see him. They were both awed and envious that one of their colleagues had the courage to give up the security of teaching. "In their eyes," Bob Page said,

"I was about to enter the glamorous world of publishing."

Actually, textbook editing is not the most inspiring craft. Unlike the trade-book editor who may deal with twenty to thirty different works a year, the textbook editor may spend three consecutive years rewriting and editing just one textbook series. And if he is unlucky he will begin all over again working on the revision as soon as he has completed the teacher's guide. Indeed, it frequently happens that an editor may spend his entire career endlessly revising Dick and Jane or a series of elementary social studies texts.

What romance and adventure exists in the industry usually befalls the textbook salesman who may either be a consultant-teacher, often a woman, or book salesman. The consultant travels around the country visiting schools where she frequently takes over classes and shows teachers how to use the firm's schoolbooks and manuals. Scott, Foresman, with the biggest staff, has forty such master teacher saleswomen on its payroll.

The consultants often work in tandem with the regular textbook salesmen whose job is to sell the books to the schools. A large firm employs as many as 100 to 150 such salesmen, who are each given a territory usually consisting of a big city or a state. The great majority are men and, in contrast to their former male teaching colleagues, more aggressive. Also because many of their customers are women, particularly in the elementary schools, schoolbook publishers somehow always seem to hire salesmen who exude a rugged masculinity.

"The guy I look for," explained D. C. Heath's Sturtevant Hobbs, who heads a national sales force of over 130 men, "must be a hungry salesman on the one hand and an articulate, tactful educator on the other. Of course this is where the conflict comes in. Our people are not in there to make a quick sale and then get the hell out. Every book or series is good for some school somewhere but not every school every-where. Our salesmen must show discretion and not foist off an article when it won't work. We may jeopardize a far more important sale next year or the year after that."

Because many textbook salesmen spend a total of three to six months of the year on the road, Heath, like other firms, seeks out men who are married. The regional managers also question the wives to find out whether they feel they could take their husband's repeated absences from home. While the salesman's salary is not that large—it ranges from $7,000 to $15,000 a year—he does receive a number of fringe bene-fits, including a liberal expense account and the use of a company car. "He does not eat in Pavillon," explained Hobbs. "But he does not spend every night in the White Tower either."

Like most traveling salesmen, the school bookman faces long periods of loneliness, which are heightened by the fact that he may spend a whole week traveling around to the schools, doing a superb job of describing his company's products, yet failing to make a single sale because the schools already have all the textbooks they need and do not plan to adopt new ones for several years.

"He is not like the Fuller Brush man," Hobbs said, "who starts out on Monday with a trunk full of brushes and comes back on Friday with an empty car. The school salesman who returns at the end of the week without taking an order has no way of telling the boss or little woman, 'Look at me. I'm a super salesman.' As a result, some textbook salesmen get very frustrated." To ease his frustrations, the Heath bookman is expected to phone a supervisor at least once a week for guidance and reassurance. These phone calls also provide a check on whether the traveling salesman is doing his job.

To see how a salesman works let us join Carl Procaskey, a Harcourt, Brace & World bookman, as he makes his rounds.

A darkly handsome man, Procaskey has been selling books for Harcourt for the past fifteen years. As a salesman of junior- and senior-high-school textbooks, he covers a territory containing 8,750 square miles and 185 school systems, ranging from the rich plum of the city of Detroit to suburban Grosse Pointe and a handful of communities in rural Michigan.

Like most school bookmen, Procaskey puts in a murderous working day. He usually arises at 6:30 A.M. and by 7 A.M. is answering phone calls from teachers or department heads seeking free samples of a schoolbook they saw displayed at a recent education meeting. By 7:30 A.M. he is on the road, driving up to a hundred miles a day. Sometimes he will travel thirty miles to make a three-minute sales pitch to a teacher who may keep him waiting an hour because she is either in class or attending a teachers' conference. Because he works in an open territory where each school or system adopts its own books, he must be constantly checking with teachers, department heads, and their secretaries to learn when his customers are ready to buy a new math or history text. Since he is competing with salesmen from thirty other companies, he is always trying to get the edge by displaying his wares which he carries around in a brown leather carrying case. The case when filled weighs about forty-five pounds and he walks two to three miles with it every day. In the evenings he is continually filling out sales reports and order forms in his basement office or in a motel room. At forty-three, Carl Procaskey usually puts in a fourteen-hour day that would exhaust a sandhog. Yet he would have it no other way. Of all the jobs he has ever held, clarinet player, shoe salesman, refrigerator inspector, grade-school teacher, selling textbooks gives him both a good living and a sense of dignity. "We must always remember," he says, "that we are the salesmen and the educators are the professionals. But this does not mean that we have to show a Uriah Heep type of obsequiousness."

As it happens to all schoolbook salesmen, the most nerve-racking moments in Carl Procaskey's life occur when he is called to appear before a textbook selection committee. On this typical Saturday he was scheduled to meet eight teachers representing four junior-high schools. The teachers had to choose the single American history textbook their eighth-grade students would use for the next five years.

It was 3:45 P.M. when the Harcourt salesman eased himself into a seat at the head of the large, oblong table. He knew that the teachers were serving on their own time without pay, that they had been listening to his competitors since 8:45 A.M., and that by this hour they were near exhaustion. From past experience he assumed that the teachers had not actually read most of the texts. Because they had to choose from among fifteen different histories and an equal number of manuals, they only had time to sample several chapters, examine the chapter and unit heads to see how the texts were organized, and to check some of the teaching suggestions in the manuals.

Rising, Carl Procaskey launched into his presentation. He used no notes and his voice combined both a folksy, friendly quality and that special ring of authority and expertise which salesmen always seem to possess.

"I'll not belabor the obvious," he began. "*The Story of the American Nation* is a real good book. Let's first look at the relative balance. Take the period up to 1865. This includes six units, or four hundred pages, or sixty percent of the book. This means we are emphasizing early American history. But of course we are not committing ourselves to cutting off the period after the 1860's."

Pausing, Procaskey searched for an approving nod. The teachers, however, seemed to be waiting for something more. "You will also find the characteristics of the book quite different," he went on. "For instance, look at the way it is organized. All the chapters are divided into numbered lessons. In terms of a teaching plan, each lesson makes up a day's work. You also will notice that each question has its own identification and comprehension questions. Also you will find at the end of each unit suggestions for short-attention-span and long-term projects."

Several heads began to nod in agreement and the Harcourt salesman swung into his peroration. "To my mind," he said, "one of the most important points in *The Story of the American Nation* is that it makes clear that this country guarantees the basic human rights and that we are ruled by the consent of the governed. Are there any questions?"

"What is the vocabulary level?" one teacher asked.

This is one of the most common questions teachers raise and Procaskey is convinced it makes little sense. He dismissed it by quoting Descarte's dictum: "I think, therefore, I am."

"Descarte's words, if taken separately, are at the third-grade level," Procaskey said. "But would most eighth-graders really understand them?"

The only other question came from a teacher who wondered whether the text provided an adequate treatment of the growth of corporations. Pointing to the appropriate chapters, Procaskey declared, "I really think we do better than most books."

The answer did not satisfy the teacher, who continued his attack. Procaskey waited for the instructor to finish and then, thanking the committee, departed. "That teacher was only displaying his erudition," he said later. "It's like pneumonia. The only thing you can do is let it run its course."

For the textbook salesman the next few weeks were pure agony. "You bleed and die, waiting for the announcement of an adoption," Procaskey said. "If you are a rational human being, you know you are going to win some and lose some. But at the moment you lose it's a bitter blow. When it is not a bitter blow, you know it's time to get another job."

While Procaskey waited and worried, the teachers met again to rate the books on the basis of the authors' qualifications, the attractiveness of the type size, teachability, readability, and historical balance. At the end of this meeting, which no salesman attended, they then voted for their first choice, which was passed on to the assistant superintendent in charge of textbook selection. He in turn approved and forwarded the teachers' recommendation to the local board of education which, in this community, automatically adopts the teachers' selection.

Finally the board met. The winner was Harcourt's *The Story of the American Nation*. Carl Procaskey was elated. But winning the adoption was not the reason he gave for praising the committee, which had had only five weeks to study and evaluate more than 10,000 textbook pages. "As far as I'm concerned," he declared, "most schools get better than they have any real right to expect from the teacher committees, considering the amount of elapsed time they get to study the books and the few cases when they are given any released time."

Much like the textbook selection committee, Procaskey himself must become an expert on his own firm's junior- and senior-high texts, manuals, and teaching aids as well as the hundreds of schoolbooks put out by his competitors. During the slow summer months when school is out he is continually reading and rereading texts on every conceivable subject from psychology and economics to physics, grammar, and algebra. "A vast majority of textbooks have a great deal in common," Procaskey said. "For instance, you can go for long stretches reading an American history and all you can say is it is a history, which is not a very distinctive thing to say. The real trick, of course, is to find out what is really different, what really grabs me. Then I look at the competition."

There are occasions, however, when Procaskey's big problem is to sell a textbook so different in its approach that the schools naturally resist buying it. "The best way for me to illustrate this is with a story," he began. "The head of a dog-food company decided he would put out the best dog food ever made. He got the best scientists to prepare it. Then he got all the salesmen together and told them to sell the hell out of the dog food. A year passed and all the salesmen met again. 'How come,' the sales manager asked, 'you guys can't sell this dog food? You know it's the best on the market.' There was a long silence. Finally one fellow raised his hand. 'I'll tell you,' he said. 'It's because the dogs won't eat the damned stuff.'

"The moral," said Procaskey, "is that the best book and the best seller are not always synonymous."

Sometimes, of course, the difference between one school-book and another has nothing to do with the quality of the texts. Once, the Harcourt salesman recalls, the teachers were repelled by a seventh-grade geography. Something had gone wrong with the glue used in the binding. "The odor was awful," Procaskey said. "So all the salesmen were instructed to tell the teachers, 'If you smell anything, it's me.' "

"I guess," he added with a grin, "we sort of turned ourselves into burnt offerings."

It sometimes happens, of course, that one of Procaskey's competitors does come out with an innovation that completely defies tradition. Such was the case when Scott, Foresman revised *England in Literature*, a twelfth-grade anthology, by replacing *Macbeth* with *Hamlet*. "In terms of merchandising," Procaskey explained, "it was a very radical move indeed."

Ever since the early 1920's *Macbeth* has been the only Shakespearean play to appear in the hardbound English anthologies used by seniors in high school. There were two reasons why the publishers chose *Macbeth*. Because it had all the elements of a blood-and-thunder Elizabethan Western the students would stand a better chance of understanding it. It also possessed the singular virtue of being the shortest of the Bard's tragedies, and since these anthologies attempt to cover the entire range of English literature from the Venerable Bede to Dylan Thomas, it could be argued that the inclusion of *Macbeth* helped save precious space.

Leo Kneer, the general editor of Scott, Foresman's junior- and senior-high-school literature department, was well aware that by switching *Hamlet* for *Macbeth* he might anger a number of teachers who would be in the disconcerting position of having to learn a new work.

"Back in 1958," Kneer said, "I toured a number of southern schools and I asked the teachers if they would use *Hamlet* instead of *Macbeth*. 'What,' they asked, 'will we do with the old books?' I suggested that they keep them. You know, there were as many as one hundred and fifty copies of *Macbeth* in some of those rooms. Then I said, 'If we give you *Hamlet*, you'll have two choices, two plays.' They seemed to think that was a good idea."

But Kneer and his fellow editors did not stop there. They also toured schools along the East and West Coasts where they discovered that many teachers were using paperback or library books to teach *Hamlet* as well as *Macbeth*. These findings were further confirmed when Scott, Foresman received the replies to five hundred *Macbeth* vs. *Hamlet* questionnaires it had sent to schools throughout the country. Despite the comment of one salesman who felt that Hamlet's "misbehaving mother" might not be accepted in the clay hills of Georgia, Scott, Foresman made the switch. Finally, in 1963, exactly 360 years after the First Quarto was published, the Prince of Denmark entered the American classroom under the official sanction of a major hardbound textbook anthology.

In Chicago, Robert C. McNamara, Jr., Scott, Foresman's director of market research, explained the economic risks involved in making publishing history. "The inclusion of *Hamlet*," he said, "was in part a commercial decision, and that is fundamental in publishing. After a while, you know, the teacher gets tired of teaching the little goose girl. It's that same damned old story again. Yes, a good case can be made for novelty. That's where *Hamlet* comes in. But if a story or a play turns out to be a real clinker, then you can end up with one hundred thousand textbooks sitting in a warehouse. Then you have a real headache."

Back in Detroit, Carl Procaskey was barreling along in a 1965 Ford Galaxie describing how he defends Harcourt's *Adventures in English Literature* which still offers *Macbeth* against Scott, Foresman's *England in Literature* which now presents *Hamlet*. He began by recalling the scene, a hot, stuffy teachers' lounge in a suburban Detroit high school. The head of a high-school English department was sitting on a brown leather couch, explaining that he has been teaching *Macbeth* for the past eighteen years and had come to hate the play with a passion.

"I can only give you two minutes," the head of the English department said. "All these papers to correct."

"I appreciate that, sir," Procaskey replied. "And time is important. As you know far better than I, your teachers have to cover so much in one year. The Anglo-Saxon Age, the Medieval Period, The Elizabethan Age, the Seventeenth

Century. Well, if you put in *Hamlet*, which is twenty percent longer than *Macbeth* . . ."

"I know. But I still prefer *Hamlet*."

"I understand," Procaskey continued. "But *Macbeth* really is more popular. And there is so much more action. I know your bright students will understand the symbolism in *Hamlet*. But will the others?"

The teacher was silent, obviously unconvinced. Dipping into his bag of sample textbooks, Procaskey pulled out a slim paperback anthology containing *Hamlet* and three other Shakespearean plays.

"Well, sir," he said, "here is a way of teaching both."

The English department chairman sadly shook his head. "You know our school budget won't allow it."

Just then a faint buzzing sound erupted in Carl Procaskey's pants pocket. It was the alarm on a parking-meter timer the Harcourt salesman used as a way of reminding himself that the two minutes the teacher had given him were up. Though he had already driven forty miles, visited three schools, and had yet to eat lunch, Carl Procaskey somehow managed to smile as he left.

CHAPTER *4*

Please Don't Eat the Money

THE MAIN LABORATORIES of the privately owned United States Testing Company, Inc., are housed in a five-story building located in the midst of Hoboken's grimy factory district. Here manufacturers from all over the country have their products tested for quality or durability. The products, which may be boiled, ground up, stretched, or shrunk, include almost everything Americans consume or use, from food and soaps to electronic components.

About ten years ago United States Testing Company began investigating the modern version of a product whose antecedents can be traced to Colonial America. Amid the surrounding sounds and smells emitted by the Hostess Cake Company, the Todd Shipyard, a Tootsie Roll factory, and Lightfoot Schultz, a soap manufacturer, U. S. Testing began to rip up dozens of textbooks to see why so many of them tended to fall apart in children's hands. For the next three years technicians conducted over two thousand different tests, checking bindings, inks, paper, and covers. There were tests for crocking (to see whether the colored dyes on the covers would rub off on boys' shirts and girls' blouses), a

Fade-O-Meter test (to show whether colored book covers faded in the sunlight), durability tests for communities with sub-zero temperatures, flexing resistance or repeated folding tests. The ultimate in simulating the rough treatment textbooks can receive in the hands of schoolchildren was the tumbling test.

"We began with this old washing machine," explained Russell Armitage, associate director of research. "We would put the books in the washing machine and the drums would whirl around. We did this to test the bindings. But we have our own special tumbling machine now and don't use the washing machine for books any more. Instead, we are using it for laundry."

Armitage, who has devoted a good part of the past decade to ripping, pounding, and smashing schoolbooks, was obviously proud of his firm's latest version of the tumbling test. In order to see the newest model a visitor entered a large, darkened room whose floor was covered with mattresses. Machines were methodically running 270-pound rollers over the mattresses, which under the impact of the rollers went "Heeya, Heeya," like the groaning wail of some overworked beast of burden.

"And here," Russell Armitage beamed, "is the tumbler." A large octagon-shaped drum consisting of steel and oak walls and a jutting shelf was turning around and around. Inside were several copies of D. C. Heath's *Handbook of English*. As the drum whirled, the textbooks would flap on their spines, going "plop, plop."

"Sometimes," interrupted Russell Armitage, "we try to wear books out by putting tape around the front edge and having the books fall end over end or on their sides. It can take as many as two thousand five hundred revolutions before the books come apart."

Back in his private office, Armitage explained that naturally no one at U. S. Testing is concerned with the readability or content of the books they test. "What we are concerned with," he declared, "is durability. Schools want textbooks to last three years. What we've done is work up standards which the Book Manufacturers Institute has adopted and which all book manufacturers must follow."

In part as a result of the Fade-O-Meter, tumbler, and other tests, the American textbook produced today is probably the sturdiest in the world. Because it is sold in massive numbers and is used nationwide it must endure a typical schoolchild's rough handling and the vagaries of regional climates from the humid south to the frozen reaches of the north.

As a product consciously concocted for the national market, the textbook must also reflect the broadest cultural and social level of the American schoolchild. This means that the textbook publisher will omit material or works which might possibly stir up regional or community prejudices or offend a particular group's point of view. Thus no hardbound literary anthology used in high school contains Shakespeare's *Othello,* because publishers are convinced that they would lose part of the southern market which would reject a school-book that had a play about "miscegenation." Similarly, no hardbound literary anthology contains *The Merchant of Venice,* because it might offend the city or suburban communities that have a large Jewish population. In addition to omitting literary works which may cause trouble, publishers leave out information or change passages and illustrations which may be considered controversial. Not long ago an artist had included a picture of a cow about to calf in a fifth-grade social-studies text. The art director took one look at the pregnant beast and ordered the illustrator to lop several hundred pounds of beef. "It is against company policy," he explained, "to show pregnancy in animals."

Finally, because mass sales are the goal, textbooks tend to sink to a level of intellectual blandness. A description of the final product appears in *High School English Textbooks,* an exhaustive survey of schoolbooks used in teaching secondary-school English. For instance, most literary anthologies studied in the ninth and tenth grades are organized topically instead of chronologically. As the authors, Professors James J. Lynch and Bertrand Evans note, topical organization is frequently employed to make literature palatable to the adolescent mind.

In *Ourselves and Others,* a tenth-grade anthology, Lynch and Evans report, "Shakespeare's 'O Mistress Mine' appears in a unit titled 'The Social Swing,' an assignment that both slights the intrinsic nature of the song and ignores its context in *Twelfth Night,* where Sir Andrew, when given a choice, specifically requests Feste to sing of love, for, as he says, 'I care not for good life.' The classification of Dickens's 'A Christmas Carol' [in *Expanding Literary Interests,* a ninth-grade anthology] as a story of 'Home Life' leaves little room for either its chief character or its central meaning. One of the strangest selections in the unit 'America Is Neighborliness,' in *America Today,* an eleventh-grade anthology, is Shirley Jackson's short story, 'The Lottery,' whose characters must surely be among the most unneighborly neighbors to be found in literature! . . ."

In their study the authors also note that only a little more than half the dramas represented in the anthologies can be classified as stage plays. Most of the others are either radio or TV plays, with an occasional sprinkling of musical comedies. "Many choices," the authors comment, "seem to have been determined by quite irrelevant criteria: introduction to television and radio, teen-age mores, the celebration of holidays, and—most frequently—'entertainment,' rather than literary quality and permanence. Shakespeare is given the greatest amount of space—twenty-seven appearances of five plays, including excerpts, abridgements, and adaptations*—but in all the anthologies examined this greatest of all writers in the English language nevertheless is given only 4.1 percent of their total space—*only one-sixth the attention given to miscellaneous and largely nonliterary prose.* It should also be remembered that in forty-five volumes (62.5 percent of the total) Shakespeare's plays are not represented at all."

One tenth-grade anthology included the musical *The King and I,* apparently, say the authors, because it had been a box-office smash. Perhaps the publisher considered an exegesis of the musical as excellent preparation for the revival of such literary events as *Annie Get Your Gun* and *Oklahoma,* but it would hardly serve the youngster who eventually is exposed to *Doctor Faustus* or even *Who's Afraid of Virginia Woolf?*

In their summary Lynch and Evans offer little encouragement to the serious students, much of whose humanistic education during the crucial years of fifteen to eighteen is based on textbook anthologies. In a section entitled "The Fear of Difficulty," the two professors report that as they examined the anthologies they were repeatedly reminded of an analogy to "instant" package food, the kind that one just "pops into the oven and serves."

"The emphasis on the 'enjoyment' of reading," they continue, "is so great in many of the anthologies as to suggest that editors have become fearful of including selections that require any effort to understand. Yet the real enjoyment of literature is a goal of reading, a goal that is reached by study; it is not a superficial 'attractiveness' necessarily apparent at

---

* The classic Shakespearean adaptations—and abominations—are: "Tomorrow and tomorrow and tomorrow, creep on, day by day, to the end of time," and "Friends, Romans, countrymen, listen to me."

the outset. We have assumed throughout this survey that anthologies are textbooks, *to be studied in and taught from,* not do-it-yourself readers in which the teacher makes assignments but takes little further responsibility. Hence we believe that most anthologies seriously underestimate the ability of students and teachers to cooperate in the thoughtful examination of important and distinguished texts, and that when difficulty exists the importance and distinction of the work at hand are sufficient justification of any effort necessary to overcome it. In the words of the Literature Committee of the School and College Conference, 'The books that really need interpretation will work best in the classroom.' Literature worth including in the anthologies often will not be 'instant' literature to heat and serve."

As in the teaching of literature, so in the teaching of the social sciences and reading the content frequently suggests *mass culture education,* which, in fairness to the publisher, is the level often set by the schools themselves.* (There are, of course, teachers and school administrators who are appalled by such standards, but they apparently are still in the minority.) In order to provide the *mass culture education* which it seems the majority of educators demand, the textbook publisher frequently makes sure that the intellectual content of schoolbooks does not surpass the broadest, and often the lowest, level of student-teacher interest and ability. As a result a cycle is created whereby the minimal standards suggested by the schools are satisfied by the textbook publisher who by issuing the schoolbooks insures that these minimal standards are maintained. The publisher is not without blame since he abets the schools in order to achieve the largest sales possible and the considerable profits which often ensue. The ultimate tragedy is that the schools, which should

* The exceptions, which will be discussed later, are mathematics, foreign languages, and high-school science.

set the highest educational standards, become the anvil upon which the intellectual content of education is shattered.

Although there are exceptions, the central dominating axiom that is responsible for most textbook publishing decisions can be found by turning to one of the industry's most brilliant and candid spokesmen, William Jovanovich, the dark-haired son of a Montenegrin coal miner who became president of Harcourt, Brace, one of the country's publishing giants, at the age of thirty-four. Now forty-five, urbane, articulate, and tough, Jovanovich also runs the Harcourt elementary- and high-school book division, edits or advises ten trade authors a year including James Gould Cozzens, Mary McCarthy, and Lewis Mumford, and currently is writing a book with Dr. Marshall McLuhan of the University of Toronto on the effects of media on concepts of authorship and publishing. In his office on the ninth floor of the Harcourt, Brace & World office building in New York, Jovanovich has surrounded himself with his favorite op and modern art, a teak dining table, a Sony TV set, and a terrace that overlooks a corner of the U.N. In his first book, *Now, Barabbas,* sections of which he first read to the Harcourt salesmen and a group of security analysts, Jovanovich summed up the single most important fact in textbook publishing.

"It may be wondered," he wrote, "why all publishers do not undertake to issue textbooks. The reasons are not complicated: some of them lack interest, others lack the skill, and most of them lack the money. Textbooks require an immense investment in capital."

Paradoxically, textbook publishers, despite soaring sales and profits, face a formidable financial problem every time they bring out a new textbook. The problem comes into sharp focus by simply comparing the economic risks involved in publishing a popular biography of George Washington sold through bookstores and an American history textbook sold directly to high schools. The publisher of the biography will employ the talents of one author, one editor, and one artist for the book's cover. He probably will recoup all his costs, including editorial, printing, and advertising, by selling about 11,000 copies and collecting $35,000.

In contrast, the same publisher can easily risk over $500,000 in producing a new eleventh-grade American history textbook. About one-third of this sum will pay for the writing, editing, and artwork. The book itself might consist of 896 pages, including a hundred specially prepared two-color maps, eight pages of four-color maps, thirty-five drawings, numerous art reproductions, graphs, and charts. Though only half the space in the book will be devoted to the text, this one-volume history will contain 300,000 words, or three times as many words as a solid nonfiction book sold to the bookstores. Every word, sentence, and historical fact will be checked for clarity or accuracy by at least two editors who will devote three years each to the text and layout. Whenever a new concept like mercantilism is mentioned, one editor will either insert the definition if it is missing or tell one of the two authors to do so. Another editor will go over the manuscript with the cartographer to insure that every place name, battle scene, and geographical location mentioned in the text also appears on the maps. To insure that the picture reproduction and text layout are as distinctive as the pages of an art magazine, the publisher will spend $75,000 on plates, typesetting, and galley changes.

As the editors and authors complete their work, the promotion and sales departments will begin publicizing the text to all the high schools that teach American history. To interest the teachers who each year instruct approximately 2,000,000 eleventh graders in United States history, they will freely give away 10,000 copies of the book. (In contrast, a trade-book publisher might give away 300 copies to reviewers and the beaters of the publicity drums. Moreover, a sale of 10,000 copies in trade is considered highly respectable.) They will also budget $115,000 for direct-mail and educational-journal advertising and salesmen's salaries and expenses. An additional $160,000 will go for the printing of 100,000 copies which the publisher must sell at $5 apiece if he intends to get his money back. In sum, a publisher of a new American history text will spend half a million dollars before selling a single copy of his book.

While the gamble in high-school publishing is enormous, the risk soars in grade-school publishing. In secondary school a youngster usually spends one year studying biology, algebra, English literature, or world history. In grade school a child devotes six years to reading, math, social studies, and general science. Since the schools expect to get a program that logically carries a child from the first through the sixth grade, the publisher must produce at least six textbooks in each subject, including one schoolbook for each grade.

In fact, he frequently must come up with much more. For instance, Ginn's basic reading series, which covers the first six grades, consists of eighty-nine different items, including eleven basic readers, seven programed texts on phonics and comprehension, twenty children's novels and short-story collections, nineteen workbooks, seventeen teacher's manuals, and an assortment of film strips, records, word cards, and charts. For each series he issues, the grade-school publisher will frequently employ twenty editors, five authors, and sometimes as many as forty free-lance artists. He may, as Addison-Wesley did when it brought out its new math series, give away 175,000 textbooks to interested teachers and schools. In short, if a new line of textbooks proves unacceptable to the grade schools, a publisher might lose as much as $3,000,000, the sum it costs to launch an elementary reading or math series.

To avoid such risks a publisher tries to develop a sixth sense that will tell him what kinds of books will prove acceptable to the schools in the next five to ten years, the amount of time it usually takes him to produce a new textbook or series or completely revise an old one. In some subjects like reading, social studies, history, and literature, he knows he cannot produce textbooks that are too different. These subjects have been taught the same way for the past thirty years because teachers were trained by the teachers colleges and the school textbooks to teach them that way.

Thus almost all new elementary social-studies series reflect the traditional spiral approach that starts with the family in the first grade and then in succeeding grades covers the school, the community, the state, the nation, and finally the world. Almost all world and American history texts are still organized chronologically, and so are most major anthologies. At the same time a revolution has taken place in the training of teachers in high-school science and foreign languages and secondary- and grade-school math, and as a result the traditional textbooks in these fields are no longer acceptable in many schools.

"You've got to be provocative, interesting, and different," explained Heath executive Sidney Gleason, "but not so different that your text is no longer standard. The problem also becomes complicated because of the velocity of change in education. When the new Physical Science Study Committee high-school physics was published, it immediately made all the other physics books out of date. I know of one publisher who had to scrap a new physics text that was just about to go to the printer. Bringing out a new text is like shooting ducks. Sometimes when you go out hunting, you find the ducks have already flown away."

In his attempt to make sure the ducks are there to be shot and plucked, the textbook publisher asks himself two questions: How far should he go in presenting a new way of teaching a subject, and what concepts would prove offensive to the schools and communities that buy his books? While there are some exceptions, most textbook publishers consciously eschew experimental approaches to learning and reject the controversial thought or work. As Lee C. Deighton, a top executive at Crowell-Collier and Macmillan, put it, "Ford can only stand one Edsel in a generation. Like Ford, the textbook publisher can't afford very many Edsels."

CHAPTER 5

The Mathematician Who Refused to Count

FOR EVERY AXIOM about textbook publishing there is always at least one exception and such an exception is George Russell, whose greatest achievement as a schoolbook editor lies in the fact that he pursued a belief almost to the point of financial disaster. Russell directs the mathematics department of Scott, Foresman, a highly traditional and financially successful grade-school publisher. Precise and gentle in manner, George Russell is a mathematical humanist who views the teaching of division and logarithms in terms of childhood agony and joy. He is also a revolutionary. For George Russell was one of the first to pioneer the new math over a decade ahead of its time. In doing so, he not only rescued thousands of young minds from years of stupefying drudgery, but he was instrumental in helping prepare this generation for the awesome calculations of the technological age.

"Beginning around nineteen thirty-two," Russell said, "teachers, school supervisors, even university people began to sense something was wrong. What we were teaching then was computation and rules. For instance, a child who was learning long division went through the rule of division, then the rule of multiplication, then the rule of comparison, then the rule of subtraction, then the rule of comparison, then the rule to bring down. There were rules for everything and a separate lesson for every little piece of skill."

Consequently, a mathematical ennui pervaded the schools, where it was unlikely that a young Archimedes, Newton, or Gauss would find inspiration. As for the ordinary citizen, his mathematical education was such that he could just manage to count out change and fill in the income-tax form. "Even the teachers," Russell recalled, "were incapable of figuring out the percentage of classroom attendance."

Starting in the early 1930's, the Scott, Foresman math editor became aware that the emphasis on rules and calculation would no longer suffice in a society whose technological complexities would increase in a geometric progression. Moreover, because there would be so much to learn, no youngster could absorb all the rules and axioms. "We had to have meaning, not just the what, but the why," Russell said.

In 1941, George Russell, who once had refused to go on for a doctorate because he thought the courses were worthless, decided to see whether the teaching of math could be drastically changed. He teamed up with two potential authors, Maurice Hartung, then associate professor of education and math at the University of Chicago, and Henry Van Engen, at the time head of the mathematics department at Iowa State Teachers College. For the next four years the three men met on weekends at the Hotel Pearson in Chicago.

"We hired a room," Russell said, "put in a blackboard, and tried to figure out a way of teaching such things as why division works. We would argue about points that no mathematician was concerned with. For instance, a mathematician would not bother to think about the difference between a fraction and a ratio. To our amazement we had a difficult time digging out the difference."

These three men hoped they could somehow crawl inside a child's mind and rediscover how he viewed the world so that they could eventually relate the child's view of reality to mathematical concepts. "A child," Russell went on, "lives in a physical world filled with objects. Mathematics is an abstract world, apart from all these objects. We wanted to move the child to the abstract world so that he need not have to associate with the physical world."

By the end of World War II, Russell had decided that the team was capable of producing a dramatic new math series. "I thought it would take us ten years to do," he said. "We didn't have the Carnegie Foundation and their millions to help." The work was painstakingly slow. The first-grade text came out in 1948, the second-grade text in 1951, the third-grade in 1953. "We couldn't make books any faster than we could think," Russell explained. In addition to producing radically new schoolbooks for children (the first-grade book consisted entirely of pictures and numbers), the math team also had to work out ways of teaching the teachers. To achieve this goal they wrote extensive teacher's guidebooks. For instance, the second-grade text the children used contained only 216 pages, but the teacher's manual that explained it totaled 748 pages.

So far no one at Scott, Foresman had seriously questioned what Russell was up to. But the math team's slow pace finally began to worry Willis Scott, then president. Scott was well aware that while an elementary school might be willing to experiment with a new math series for grades one through six, it was unlikely to invest in "a crazy new approach" to math that abruptly halted at the fourth grade. One day Scott called Russell into his office. "You know how much you have already cost us?" Scott asked. "Six hundred thousand dollars!"

"I was kind of glad he said that," Russell recalled. "Actually I had already cost the company three-quarters of a million dollars."

The head of the math department resolved that the only logical way he could get his project out of the red was to go deeper into debt. He proceeded to do just that by doubling his editorial staff on the theory that more editors would mean faster book production. "Management was like the patient and I was the doctor," Russell said. "They took me on faith."

Not surprisingly, the public looked upon the new Scott, Foresman math books with more than passing skepticism. "They thought we were crazy," Russell recalled, adding somewhat ruefully, "Today [a decade later] they say we are not modern enough."

Despite his detractors, the textbook editor was convinced that the new math would be the wave of the future. "What I was worried about," he said, "was whether it would come fast enough to save our lives." To win over parents and teachers, the textbook publisher launched a major publicity campaign which included an elaborate color film explaining what the new math was about, special public-relations kits for the schools, and extensive newspaper publicity.

Typical of the problems that challenged the ingenuity of Russell and his fellow mathematicians was how do you get youngsters to understand what long division is all about. Under the old method schoolchildren were frequently stumped by division because all they were given were rote techniques developed as short-cut methods for mathematicians who already understood what they were doing. In effect, the traditional method forced young children, all of whom were beginners, to work at maximum proficiency.

Under the new system a youngster in the fourth grade is presented with the following lesson on division:

Learning how

This lesson shows how to divide when the numeral for the divisor has two figures.

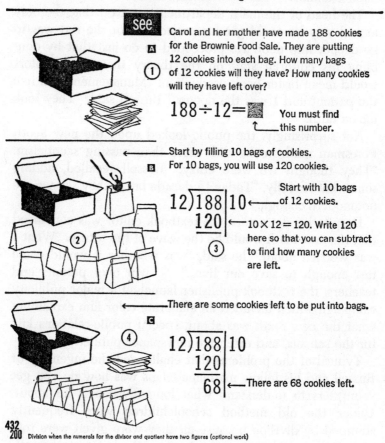

see

A

(1) Carol and her mother have made 188 cookies for the Brownie Food Sale. They are putting 12 cookies into each bag. How many bags of 12 cookies will they have? How many cookies will they have left over?

$$188 \div 12 = \blacksquare$$

You must find this number.

B

Start by filling 10 bags of cookies. For 10 bags, you will use 120 cookies.

Start with 10 bags of 12 cookies.

$$12)\overline{188}\ \big|\ 10$$
$$\ \ 120$$

(3) 10 × 12 = 120. Write 120 here so that you can subtract to find how many cookies are left.

(2)

C

There are some cookies left to be put into bags.

(4)

$$12)\overline{188}\ \big|\ 10$$
$$\ \ 120$$
$$\ \ \ \ 68$$

There are 68 cookies left.

Division when the numerals for the divisor and quotient have two figures (optional work)

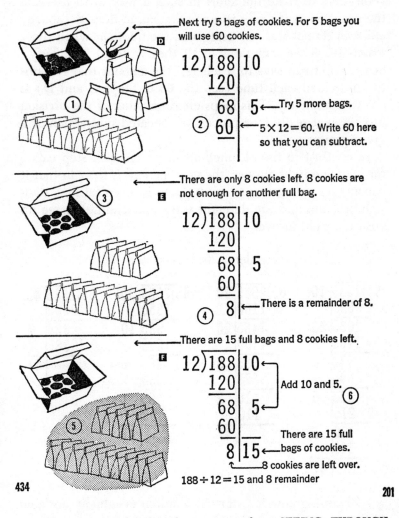

Next try 5 bags of cookies. For 5 bags you will use 60 cookies.

D

$$
\begin{array}{r|l}
12)\overline{188} & 10 \\
120 & \\
\hline
68 & 5 \longleftarrow \text{Try 5 more bags.} \\
② \;\; 60 & \longleftarrow 5 \times 12 = 60. \text{ Write 60 here} \\
& \quad\text{so that you can subtract.}
\end{array}
$$

There are only 8 cookies left. 8 cookies are not enough for another full bag.

E

$$
\begin{array}{r|l}
12)\overline{188} & 10 \\
120 & \\
\hline
68 & 5 \\
60 & \\
\hline
④ \;\; 8 & \longleftarrow \text{There is a remainder of 8.}
\end{array}
$$

There are 15 full bags and 8 cookies left.

F

$$
\begin{array}{r|l}
12)\overline{188} & 10 \longleftarrow \\
120 & \qquad\qquad \text{Add 10 and 5.} \;\; ⑥ \\
\hline
68 & 5 \longleftarrow \\
60 & \\
\hline
8 & 15 \longleftarrow \text{bags of cookies.} \\
& \quad\;\; \text{There are 15 full}
\end{array}
$$

8 cookies are left over.

$188 \div 12 = 15$ and 8 remainder

434

201

Lesson pages reprinted with permission from SEEING THROUGH ARITHMETIC 4 by Maurice L. Hartung, Henry Van Engen and Lois Knowles, Copyright © 1956, 1961, 1963 by Scott, Foresman and Company, Glenview, Illinois.

Among other things, this method makes it possible for youngsters to write numerals in such a way as to describe the situation as it really is. For example, in Step B (above) children do not start by using 1 in the quotient when the 1 means 10. When they think of 10, they write 10. "Similarly," Scott, Foresman says to teachers, "the amount that remains to be divided each time (see the 68 in Steps C and D) is shown completely. This helps children think of the division process as it really is—a process of repeated subtraction of a given group."

In contrast to the old method in which each step called for only one right answer, the new method is freer in that it encourages youngsters to guess. Here is a typical long division problem and the different ways four children came up with the right answer.

Problem: 2585 ÷ 55 = ?

```
55)2585 10     55)2585 20     55)2585 30     55)2585 40
    550             1100           1650           2200
   2035 20         1485 20         935 10          385 7
   1100            1100            550             385
    935 10          385 5          385 6               47
    550             275            330
    385 5           110 2           55 1
    275             110             55
    110 2               47             47
    110
        47
```

By learning how to estimate, children eventually are able to do long division in their heads. Moreover, they are learning to solve mathematical problems more quickly at earlier ages. For example, says George Russell, in 1942 only bright seventh graders (about 15 percent of a typical class) could divide 84,523 by 24. Today, he says, youngsters with low-average intelligence are solving the same problem in the fifth grade.

For Russell and his colleagues solving the problems involved in writing new math textbooks had taken twenty-three years, from 1941, when they first began working in the Pearson Hotel, until 1964, when the publisher could announce the completion of the series which continued from the first through the ninth grades. Total costs, both editorial and production, came to ten million dollars. The series began to show a profit only two years ago. Incredibly, it had taken the publisher from 1945, when it made its initial investments, to 1964—a period of nineteen years—to get its money back.

"What saved our lives," said George Russell, "was World War Two, nuclear energy, automation, Sputnik, and the School Mathematics Study Group which used federal money to upgrade the teaching of math in the schools. If these things had not happened, we would still be teaching computation by rules."

The kind of innovations that George Russell and his colleagues helped pioneer are the exceptions rather than the rule for not only Scott, Foresman but the textbook publishing industry. Robert J. R. Follet, a vice-president and general manager of the Educational Division of Follet Publishing Company, explained why. Bob Follet, at thirty-seven, may be considered a young man of conservative sensibilities, who still rides to work in a car pool and who carries his lunch in a brown paper bag.

"The trouble with the big publisher," he said during an interview in his office one Sunday, "is that he is tied to his basal titles for his profits. And because he is used to his profit structure, he can't afford to change. Let's say I was convinced that there was a better way to teach social studies.

Could I afford to abandon the series I already have? I certainly could not. It takes years to alter the teaching practices of teachers. But let's say I decide to bring out this new series. Why, I'd put myself out of business, and then it would take ten years to get it back."

Understandably, as Bob Follet suggests, it is not the obligation of the executives who run textbook houses to preside over the liquidation of their firms' assets. At the same time, to the extent to which a schoolbook publisher is accustomed to the profits it garners from its big sellers, to that same degree educational innovation and progress will be denied the schools. It is on the horns of this ancient dilemma that education has been pinned for generations.

CHAPTER *6*

Molding a Nation

OF ALL THE ARTIFACTS produced by a modern civilization, from the plumbing used by its citizens to the weapons employed by its soldiers, none compares with the schoolbook as a mirror of that civilization's aspirations and failings. Certainly in America, schoolbooks over the decades have embodied most of the nation's beliefs and prejudices. But the textbook is more than just a cultural fossil which will delight and amuse some future anthropologist. As the most important educational tool of the past and the present, the textbook is instrumental in molding the attitudes and passions of the young and thus both reflects and shapes the beliefs of the nation itself. Indeed, one may suggest that schoolbooks studied by previous generations have had an influence on the development of the American people that is almost as profound as the achievements of Thomas Jefferson, Franklin Delano Roosevelt, and Henry Ford.

As every youngster knows, American history begins with the ringing of a religious tocsin. Many of the settlers who braved the first Atlantic crossings came to the wilderness in search of religious freedom. For these grim pioneers church and state were joined, and in keeping with their narrow view of the world, education had as its sole aim the indoctrination of God's children according to the teachings of Calvin and Knox. Although the founding of the Republic eventually led to the separation of church and state, the citizens residing in New England, the South, and the West continued for many years to use education as the tool that taught children to read the Bible while instilling the tenets of a God-centered world.

Perhaps fittingly, since respect for the schoolmaster only reflected a healthy fear of the Lord, the first textbooks were shaped like paddles. Called hornbooks, these primitive devices had imprinted on them the alphabet, the benediction, and the Lord's Prayer. While the hornbook was certainly a simple text, the early colonists could be excused for failing to supply their children with better tools since nearly all books had to be imported from England. At that time the English looked upon the settlers as so much manpower which would provide them with financial gain. Consequently the mother country was unwilling to expend funds on such luxuries as books and education.

This limited vision of imperial beneficence was epitomized by Seymour, the haughty King's attorney general who in 1691 received James Blair of Virginia. Blair had sailed to England to plead for the establishment of a college, contending that by training Church of England clergymen in Virginia it would be possible to save the souls of the colonists. Seymour heard Blair out and in a fit of British spleen exclaimed, "Damn your souls, make tobacco!" As one historian notes, "But two years later, perhaps because Blair convinced the royal proprietors that saved souls could produce more tobacco than damned souls, he got the charter for William and Mary College."

Despite the general lack of encouragement from the mother country, plantation owners in Virginia were hiring private tutors for their young, and Massachusetts and other New England colonies were instituting what was to become the forerunner of the American public school. In 1647 the New England Commonwealth passed the first school law which ordered the hiring of a schoolmaster in each township with a population of at least fifty families.

The main function of the schoolmaster was to exorcise the devil. Declared the preamble to the Massachusetts' school law, "It being one chief project of that old deluder, Satan, to keep men from the knowledge of ye Scriptures," effort must be made to thwart this "old deluder that learning may not be buried in ye grave . . ."

The *New England Primer* was the first textbook of consequence to appear in the colonies and it readily met the most stringent demands of the school market of that time. Although the bibliographic details are obscure, it appears that it was originally published by Benjamin Harris, an emigré from London who first settled in Philadelphia, where he landed in the pillory and eventually in prison for issuing several tracts which distressed the English. He then moved on to Boston, setting himself up as a printer and innkeeper. Around 1690 he purportedly issued the first edition of the famous *Primer,* which he patterned after earlier English textbooks.

Like most early schoolbooks, the *New England Primer* contained all that a child needed to learn during the course of his exceedingly brief education.* Although editions varied, the *New England Primer* usually began with the alphabet invariably in verse:

A   In Adam's Fall
    We Sinned all.

* By 1800 the citizen who received formal instruction spent on the average a total of four months and two days in school. By 1840 the amount of time increased to ten months, eight days, and by 1850 totaled twenty-two months, ten days.

B   Heaven to find,
    The Bible Mind.
C   Christ Crucify'd,
    For Sinners dy'd.

Once a youngster had learned the ABC's, he was then confronted with a collection of reading matter, nearly all of which was religious in theme and form. He was given questions on Bible facts, Bible verses, prayers, the Creed and, in later editions, "Mr. Cotton's Cathechism."

Since the Puritans dwelt in constant fear of the anger of the Lord and the unseen hand of the devil, they attempted to instill in their children similar notions and terrors. In the *New England Primer,* for example, youngsters were given verses like this one to commit to memory:

Good Children must

Fear God all Day,	Love Christ alway,
Parents obey,	In secret pray,
No false things say,	Mind little play,
By no sin stray,	Make no delay

In doing Good.

Along with numerous admonitions, the *New England Primer* was preoccupied with death, often in its most grisly form. This concentration on a motif which would mortify present-day child psychologists may well have had the desirable effect of hardening the young to death itself, a constant companion in the wilderness and the colonies.

An illustration of a typical lesson is this description of the last moments in the life of John Rogers. For the Puritans, to whom bigotry was not an unnatural emotion, it had the twin virtues of damning the Catholics while praising God.

Mr. John Rogers, Minister of the Gospel in London, was the first Martyr in Queen Mary's Reign, and was burned at Smithfield, February the Fourteenth, 1554. His Wife, with nine small Children & one at her Breast, following him to the Stake, with which Sorrowful Sight he was not in the least daunted, but with wonderful Patience died courageously for the Gospel of JESUS CHRIST.

In most editions of the *New England Primer* this text was accompanied by a woodcut portraying John Rogers at the stake with spittles of flame leaping at his body. Nearby stood two enormous guards and John Rogers' wife and children, all posing as if they were attending a Sunday picnic. Curiously, every participant in this auto-da-fé was smiling. Rogers and his family were overjoyed at his martyrdom and the guards were delighted because they were burning a Protestant. According to one scholar, this woodcut was among the most popular pictures in early New England.

This depiction of Catholics burning a Protestant martyr is only one of many examples of the virulent anti-Catholicism which filled the pages of the nation's schoolbooks from pre-Revolutionary days through most of the nineteenth century. Catholicism itself was attacked as a "usurpation" of the true religion and priests were described as greedy lechers. For example, a geography, published in 1818, taught: "The monks and ecclesiastics themselves, who today will pardon your sins for a groat, tonight will become defiled with your bosom-companion in her marriage-bed. And the daughter on whom you dote, while saying her mass, will become debauched by a pretending saint!" Or children studying a reader in 1828 learned: "For many ages the Popes not only pretended to be infallible, but exalted themselves above all the kings of the earth, to the very throne of CHRIST; assuming the right of pardoning sin, and of giving or rather selling the liberty of indulging in every species of wickedness and corruption." Or this question posed in an 1866 speller: "Is papacy at variance with paganism?" Moreover, only Catholic persecutions of Protestants were described in full.

Ruth Miller Elson, in *Guardians of Tradition,* a fascinating study of nineteenth-century American schoolbooks, comments: ". . . The schoolchild in this period would associate Catholicism only with unpleasant behavior and subversive beliefs. He would imbibe not only the idea that its theology is false, but that it is inimical to industry, prosperity, knowledge, and freedom—concepts considered basic to all civilization. According to those schoolbooks published before 1870, Catholicism has no place in the American past or future, nor in the economic and political climate of the United States."

The anti-Catholicism which pervaded the public schools may explain in part why the Catholics were so intent upon establishing their own parochial institutions. In fact, before and after the founding of the Republic, the only way a Catholic parent could provide his child with a positive view of his religion was to send him to a parochial school. To meet the demands of the Catholic market, publishers began issuing two separate editions for almost every subject taught in the schools. As one editor explained it, "There are really two kinds of textbooks, the baptized or Catholic text and the public-school textbook."

In most instances, however, the differences are minor. In a current Catholic math book, for example, a child sees illustrations of a teaching nun; in a public-school text the illustration shows a lay teacher. Otherwise the texts are identical. In the John Carroll edition of the *Rise of the American Nation* a youngster spends an additional thirty seconds reading another quarter of a page on the founding of Maryland by Catholics searching for religious freedom. He is also supplied with brief biographies of leading Catholic figures like James Cardinal Gibbons, who in 1887 prevented the church from censuring the then struggling labor movement, and Mother Katherine Drexel, the founder of the Sisters of the Blessed Sacrament. In the public-school edition Cardinal Gibbons is replaced by John Wesley Powell, a writer and western explorer, and Mother Drexel turns into Frances Perkins, F.D.R.'s Secretary of Labor and the first woman to become a member of the President's cabinet.

Except for the teaching of church doctrine, the most noticeable difference between many Catholic and public-school texts is that the authors of the Catholic texts freely express their opinions and do not hesitate to condemn injustice such as racial discrimination on the grounds that all human beings are created by God. Moreover, even when these texts deal with controversial religious themes like the Reformation, they frequently present accounts similar to those published in the public-school text. "The days of the pietistic approach when rosaries were added to rosaries instead of apples to apples are over," said James S. Donnelly, the Catholic editor at Silver Burdett and the former dean of the Fordham University School of Education.

After 1870 anti-Catholicism generally disappeared in the schoolbooks because it would seem Protestant Americans were distracted by the Civil War, westward expansion, and industrialization. However, the textbook authors of the latter part of the century failed to present positive Catholic contributions to American culture. As Miss Elson suggests, the United States remained a Protestant nation founded on Puritan principles.

In fact, Puritan values, only slightly diluted by time, continued to dominate American education into the twentieth century. Almost all the popular textbook writers of the previous century came from New England and those writers

were imbued with Puritan doctrine. Throughout the Colonial period such heady religious motifs as the burning of
John Rogers and the virtues of the Calvinistic catechism
permeated all schoolbooks. One scholar who surveyed textbooks up to the Revolution reported that 92 percent of their
content contained religious themes. After the adoption of the
Constitution and the Bill of Rights, religious content decreased and was replaced by fables, myths, and folklore
which were no less moralistic. Actually the Founding
Fathers, by granting religious freedom to all, had only taken
the first step in settling the issue of separation of church and
state. It wasn't until 1844 that New Jersey became the first
state to amend its constitution with the provision that there
should be no sectarian religious teaching in public-supported
schools.

"In practice," Mark Sullivan wrote in *Our Times* in 1927,
"all that was ended or prevented by the constitutional
amendments was any sectarian or religious teaching that
should run counter to the dogmas or practices of any important sect or creed. Religion remained in the schools to
practically as great an extent as immediately before the
amendments. What happened was that the States carried
on a system of education in which practically all the tradi-
tions and most of the influences were religious. The spirit
of the schools was religious and continued so. So deeply
imbedded was the spirit of religion in the common schools
of America that nothing short of a revolution, or a trend
immensely long, could have uprooted it. . . ."

In keeping with the religious and moral tenets of the
period, textbook writers in the nineteenth century continued
to show their preference for Christian doctrine. Their religious zeal also fostered a penchant for scientific ignorance.

As Ruth Elson notes, when Charles Darwin's *Origin of
Species* appeared in 1859, American educators were totally

unprepared to accept a theory that did not possess a teleo-
logical explanation. Although mammoth and dinosaur fossils
had been discovered in the early 1800's, their existence and
relation to living animal structure are not mentioned in
schoolbooks until the 1870's. Nor was any mention made of
the ice age until then. Moreover, Darwin's name does not
appear in any schoolbook until 1897, and then the reference
is so cryptic as to be meaningless. As we shall see in Chapter
10, this anti-Darwinian heritage is still strong enough to
censor textbooks being used in the schools today.

While constrained by their religion in their educational
endeavors, the early Americans also seemed determined to
free themselves from the cultural domination of England.
The textbook writer largely responsible for achieving this
independence was Noah Webster.

Best known as the compiler of the dictionary bearing his
name, Webster was a scholar in perpetual motion. His
talents which were many and his energy which must have
been inexhaustible allowed him to serve as a teacher, lawyer,
newspaper publisher, magazine editor, salesman, county
judge, and member of the Connecticut House of Representatives. He was responsible for some of the first copyright laws
passed by the states and compiled *A History of the United
States*. It was the first time that a schoolbook contained
authentic American historical material. He also became the
author of the famous *Blue-Backed Speller,* named after the
blue paper which was pasted over its thin oak-board covers.
Probably no single textbook has equaled the popularity of
the Webster *Speller*. Over one hundred million copies have
been sold and it still can be purchased from the American
Book Company, its most recent publisher.

"More than five generations of Americans learned from it,"
wrote Mark Sullivan in *Our Times*. "The first studied it
before there was any United States, as early as 1787; and it

was still being used in schools as late as the early 1900's. Boys learned from the *Blue-Backed Speller*, grew up, became Presidents of the United States, died, and were relatively forgotten, while the presses of D. Appleton & Company ground out new editions for second, third, and fourth generations. The first edition was printed on a hand-press, the last on the most modern Hoe; the first antedated the Presidency of Washington, the last was contemporary with [Theodore] Roosevelt."

Noah Webster's reasons for writing a textbook grew out of the special conditions the colonists faced in the midst of a revolution. In 1782, Webster, a tall, slender youth of twenty-four, was teaching at a classical school in Goshen, New York. "The country," he observed, "was impoverished, intercourse with Great Britain was interrupted and schoolbooks were hardly attainable."

More important than his desire to relieve the schoolbook shortage was Webster's plan to end Britain's cultural domination of the new nation. Although the *Speller* was patterned after two English schoolbooks popular in the colonies, Webster's own textbook for the first time contained Americanized pronunciation, syllabication, and spelling lists. He also replaced the heavy religious content of the English texts with precepts of the Poor Richard variety ("Great haste often makes waste.") while preserving a reverent tone by including several religious maxims ("An infidel is one who disbelieves in revelation."). In addition, he larded the book with a potpourri of inanities ("History is an account of past events. A great part of history is an account of men's crimes and wickedness."), anatomical descriptions ("A proboscis is a long tube or snout from the mouth or jaw."), mathematical definitions and revolutionary maxims ("Despotism is tyranny or oppressive government."), and insular observations ("It was once a practice in France to divorce husband and wife for incompatibility of tempers; a practice soon found to be incompatible with social order."). All of this was followed with a collection of fables, each with its own didactic moral.

Because the British copyright laws were no longer in force, Webster sought protection for the *Speller* by campaigning for the passage of copyright legislation in Connecticut, where he lived, and in New Jersey, New York, Massachusetts, and Pennsylvania. In 1783 two Hartford printers agreed to issue 5,000 copies of the *Speller*, though Webster had to put up a note that covered the entire risk. He thus became the author, copyright owner, and publisher and, not stopping there, traveled from town to town selling his own textbook.

The *Blue-Backed Speller* proved an almost instantaneous success. Within two years after its publication it was selling at the rate of five hundred copies a week. Various printers in Boston, Albany, New York, and Philadelphia were given contracts to reproduce the book. Because of the lack of transportation facilities, it was impossible at that time to publish a nationwide edition, and in fact the schoolbook issued for national distribution did not come into existence until the establishment of the railroads. By 1817 Webster had received $40,000 from one printer just to issue the book in his territory. In 1880, nearly a hundred years after it was first published, William H. Appleton was asked what was the best-selling book published by his firm. He replied:

Webster's *Speller;* and it has the largest sale of any book in the world except the Bible. We sell a million copies a year. Yes, and we have been selling it at that rate for forty years. The year following the emancipation of the slaves we sold one million five hundred thousand, because every negro [sic] in the South thought it only necessary to have a Webster's *Speller* to read. After that year it fell back to the original million, and has never varied. We sell them in cases of seventy-two dozen, and they are bought by all the large dry-goods houses and supply stores, and furnished by them to every cross-roads store.

Starting around 1820, the scope of education broadened and all-inclusive schoolbooks like Webster's *Speller* were supplemented or replaced by a variety of specialized texts covering different subjects and skills, such as readers, arithmetics, grammars, geographies, and histories. About two decades later textbook authors began writing or compiling series of readers containing increasingly difficult material. Also around 1840, special schools for the training of teachers were founded, although their influence was not felt until the latter part of the nineteenth century. As educators formed their own professional class, with that vested interest that always seems to accompany organized expertise, the number of textbooks written by professional writers markedly decreased. Approximately 36 percent of the schoolbooks published between 1876 and 1886 were written by professional authors. By 1926 that figure had dropped to 12 percent, and as has been noted earlier, most schoolbooks are now created by ex-teacher editors with the assistance of professional educators.

Although today's textbooks are not without their faults, at least they do not reflect to the same degree the superstitions and prejudices that permeated the schoolbooks of the past. Moreover, while textbooks continue to dominate classroom teaching, the schoolbook literally provided the education a child received during the most formative period of the nation's development. In the nineteenth century most teachers had little if any training, and as one theorist at the time suggested, a major reform could be achieved if teachers would only read the schoolbooks they gave to their students. During this era education consisted of rote learning and letter-perfect memorization. In a typical classroom the teacher relied on older students, who, acting as monitors, would take over the teacher's functions by listening to and correcting the recitation of the younger students. Thus not only general information but value judgments were drilled into the young who rarely had an opportunity to question what they were being taught.

And the sentiments absorbed by youngsters were appalling. It was in the nineteenth century that textbooks developed a racist theory of history that was applied not only to people of different skin color but to different religions and nationalities. In addition to Negroes and Indians, the Irish, Jews, Chinese, Italians, French, Arabs, and Russians were all declared inferior, the claim invariably made on racial grounds. The only nationalities praised besides the white Protestant Americans were the people of Switzerland, Scotland, Britain, Germany, and Japan, all of whom were admired for their industriousness, and in the case of the Swiss and the Scots, for their Calvinism.

The racist theory of history and people began with the Indian, who was considered both the noble savage, since he was the first to occupy the American continent, and a barbarian who stood in the way of westward expansion. According to the schoolbooks of the nineteenth century, Indians were described as "cruel," possessing a "diabolical thirst for blood" and delighting in listening "to the cries of their victims."

Indian genocide, in turn, was rationalized on the grounds that the white man represented a superior race to whom the Protestant God had given the right to occupy and cultivate the land. Typical were sentiments like this one offered by Benson John Lossing in *A Primary History of the United States,* published in 1866: "God, in his wise providence, has permitted the white man to take the Indian's land away from him. The Indian would not cut down the trees and raise grain, except here and there a little patch; but the white man, as the Bible says, has made 'the wilderness to blossom as the rose.' "

While the white man was portrayed as the superior race, the Negro throughout the nineteenth century was described as the most inferior. Indeed, racism, which filled the school-books at that time, was as virulent as the anti-Catholicism mentioned earlier. Young minds were exposed to such senti-ments as the Negroes' "mental powers, in general, participate in the imbecility of their bodies" in an 1815 reader, and Negroes are "destitute of intelligence" in an 1851 geography. "Throughout the century," writes Ruth Elson, "a direct cor-relation is assumed between darkness of color and weakness of intellect."

One of the most artful and original textbook authors writ-ing during these early years was Elijah Parish, a minister of the gospel who, in this single paragraph taken from his 1810 geography, managed to praise his own region, New England, while condemning the South, slavery, and the slaves them-selves:

We now proceed to examine another section of the country. A new shade of character commences. We shall no longer de-scribe a hardy race of industrious farmers, living together on terms of equality. Instead of the social villages of New Eng-land, and the Middle States, their highly cultivated farms, and numerous flocks, and herds, we shall discover thinly scattered farm houses, some of them miserable hovels, and a few miles distant, a lofty mansion, surrounded by 100 negro [sic] huts; some of these wretched inhabitants are in rags, some naked; some of black, and partly white; an index of their morals.

While slavery was generally frowned upon before and after the Civil War, the subject was treated in a more neutral and at times even favorable light as the great conflict approached. John A. Nietz, emeritus professor of the University of Pittsburgh and the author of *Old Textbooks*, comments, "No doubt, the desire by the authors to sell their books also in the South did much to change their treatment of slavery." *

Adds Ruth Miller Elson: ". . . The generations that made decisions about the Civil War, slavery and Reconstruction, whatever they were taught about slavery, were thoroughly indoctrinated with the idea of Negro racial inferiority. It is interesting to observe that this inferiority consists in a lack of the very qualities—responsibility, industriousness, initiative—considered particularly valuable to an American 'on the make.' Their conspicuous absence makes the Negro a poor candidate for equality in American civilization."

In contrast to the treatment of Negroes and the Catholics, the Jews at first fared somewhat better in early American textbooks. During the post-Revolutionary period they were presented, says Miss Elson, as a distinct, unpleasant religious and cultural group to be tolerated rather than accepted. However, by the end of the nineteenth century they, too, appeared as "a race" with immutable traits. Instead of praising the Jew for showing initiative and industriousness, schoolbooks portrayed him as being greedy, ambitious, and intelligent, characteristics which could only instill fear in the non-Jewish child. Jewish success, Miss Elson observes, "was

---

* Most of the schoolbooks used in the South before and after the Civil War were written by New Englanders. However, when the war cut off supplies from the North, Confederate authors began writing their own textbooks. While some continued to preach Northern doctrine, several Confederate texts took up the Southern point of view, which found its way even in the arithmetics, such as this problem posed in a Confederate text published in 1863: "If 5 white men can do as much work as 7 negroes, how many days of 10 hours each will be required for 25 negroes to do a piece of work which 30 white men can do in 10 days of 9 hours each?" Alabama, incidentally, still uses in its schools a specially prepared version of Southern history which contains a Confederate flag on the cover. In keeping with the spirit of the text, the Stars and Stripes do not appear.

viewed as Jewish subversion, and the child who imbibed values from his schoolbooks was most likely to regard the Jew as an indigestible addition to the American melting pot."

Before 1886 nearly 45 percent of the content of American history texts was concerned with war; the event which received the most space was the American Revolution. Though the causes of the Revolution were rarely explained, the rebellion was treated as an occasion similar to the Second Coming, and Washington as a Christlike figure possessed with magic powers. The super patriotism that trilled through the pages of yesterday's schoolbooks can be illustrated by this passage taken from G. P. Quackenbos' *Primary History of the United States,* published in 1869. The section was entitled:

GOING TO WAR

8. One mother fitted out her eldest son with a fowling-piece and slugs made out of her pewter spoons. Her younger boy was only sixteen. For him she had nothing but an old rusty sword. Giving him this, she dashed away a tear, and bade him follow his brother. "Beg or borrow a sword, my child," she said; "or you will find one. Some coward, I dare say, will be running away. Then take his gun and march forward."

9. At Barn-sta-ble, the only child of a farmer joined a company that was about to march to Cambridge. As they passed the father's house on leaving the village, he came forth and said: "God be with you all, my friends! and, John, if you, my son, are called into battle, take care that you behave manfully, or else let me never see your face again." This was the spirit everywhere. Twenty thousand patriots were soon in arms around Boston.

For Mark Sullivan, that delightful chronicler of the early twentieth century, it is not in the least amazing that men writing two and three generations after the Revolution should have turned this of all wars into a children's crusade. The American schoolboy of the 1870's and 1880's, and hence the generation from 1900 to 1925, lived, Sullivan wrote, "in an atmosphere as close to the Revolutionary War as if it had taken place a decade before, instead of a century," noting that American resistance to British economic and political oppression was the one great epic of our history. "Many of the writers of textbooks," he continued, "had had the story of the Revolution direct from the lips of fathers or grandfathers who had fought in it." Sullivan recounts the story told by Benjamin F. Butler, a congressman who continued as a power in Massachusetts politics until as late as 1890: "To his father's home on winter nights would come two old Revolutionary soldiers. The father and the guests would go to the cellar and draw a big pitcher of cider, which they would set in the hot ashes of the fireplace. To give further heat to the beverage they would add to it dried peppers from a string hanging above the fireplace. Fortified with this stimulus to patriotic memories, they would fix their eyes on the old musket that hung above the mantlepiece, and would rehearse the times they beat the British tyrants, to the ears of a small boy in whose mature life that story was to be a dominating influence."

As the soldiers of the Revolution retreated into the misty memories generated by Old Glory and warm cider, they left behind future generations whose fervor was relegated to a condemnation of the evils of alcohol and tobacco. Indeed, it must have been a cold and humorless age that had schoolchildren suffer through such poems as "Temperance Song," in which John Pierpont describes a flock of birds on a crisp, sunny day and then offers these lines:

Why do they twitter and sing, do you think?
Because they've had nothing but water to drink?

Or the 1844 reader which portrayed a man so sotted with alcohol that he literally explodes upon lighting his pipe. Or the schoolbook, published in 1883, that tells the tale of another drunkard who kills his son by tossing an empty wine cup out of a window. By the end of the nineteenth century numerous state legislatures had passed laws which required physiology and health textbooks to portray the evil effects of alcohol and tobacco. In order to secure book adoptions in the various states, publishers would steep their schoolbooks in all sorts of alcoholic horrors. In due course the nation went dry, and some of the credit must be given to those textbook publishers who abetted a national aberration.

As we look back on those years, we can see that the textbooks and the schools themselves held the Puritan ethic as their basic moral principal. It was this ethic that shaped and unified the nation. "The value judgment," writes Ruth Miller Elson, "is their stock in trade: love of country, love of God, duty to parents, and the necessity to develop habits of thrift, honesty, and hard work in order to accumulate property, the certainty of progress, the perfection of the United States. These are not to be questioned. Nor in this whole century of great external change is there any deviation from these basic values. In pedagogical arrangements the schoolbook of the 1790's is vastly different from that of the 1890's, but the continuum of values is uninterrupted. . . . The child is to learn ethics as he learns information about his world, unquestioningly, by rote. His behavior is not to be inner-directed, nor other-directed, but dictated by authority and passively accepted."

Thus we entered the twentieth century.

CHAPTER 7

Truman + Sex = Fear

ON APRIL 28, 1965, Dr. J. D. McAulay began mailing questionnaires to a cross-section of the nation's grade-school teachers. Dr. McAulay, a professor of elementary education at Pennsylvania State University, sought to learn how teachers in the first through sixth grades handled controversial issues in the classroom. In the questionnaire Dr. McAulay defined controversy as current events which have a strong emotional bias. Over two thousand teachers, or 77 percent of those who received the questionnaires, responded. If this survey had been conducted in Russia, China, or South Africa, we would consider the results shocking, though expected. The fact that Dr. McAulay's findings are the result of a study made in the United States can only leave one with a terrible sense of dismay. Here are some of the questions Dr. McAulay posed and the teachers' responses:

Question: Do you *initiate* a discussion of controversial issues in your classroom?
Of the 1,251 teachers who replied, 1,153, or 92 percent, said, "No."
Question: Do you *discuss* controversial issues with your children?

Of the 1,945 teachers who answered this question, 1,742, or 89 percent, said "No." *

Question: Do you *believe* you should discuss in the classroom current events topics which are controversial?

Of the 1,994 teachers who replied, 1,591, or 79 percent, said, "No."

In a similar survey conducted among 648 grade-school teachers in one eastern state, 89 percent reported to Dr. Mc-Aulay that they believed they lacked the competence to discuss controversial issues with children. "I don't know enough about such topics to feel safe," one teacher said. Replied another, "The children get quickly out of hand when we discuss something unusual like that." A third responded, "I don't think the school is the place to talk about sex and divorce and steel troubles." A fourth replied, "Well, our course of study is full enough as it is."

"It is difficult," Dr. McAulay commented, "to understand how a competent social studies teacher can escape controversial issues. If the social studies unit has any depth, creativeness, or child-centered direction, it would seem impossible for controversial issues to be side-stepped."

How, Professor McAulay asked, would it be possible for a sixth-grade unit on the Caribbean to ignore the question, "Why is Cuba in the Soviet orbit?" Or, he inquired, how could a unit on the United Nations be pertinent and alive without a sixth grader asking why a nation containing almost a third of the earth's people is not represented within the world organization? "The elementary school," he declared, "is not a cocoon. In all probability, several children in a first-grade class come from broken homes. How can a unit on the family ignore separated parents? A second-grade unit on the

---

* In a breakdown the survey also indicated that controversial issues are not discussed in schools in the South and Midwest and that such issues were discussed more widely in large city schools and less often in schools of smaller communities.

community should discuss different types of neighborhoods, the factory area, the business area, the suburb. To ignore the fact that some children live in a better section of the community than others is to ignore reality."

Moreover, to avoid such topics is to deny the youngsters themselves the opportunity of investigating the very issues which the teachers believe interest their own students. Yet, according to the nationwide survey, a number of teachers felt they could not bring the real world into the classroom. Under such circumstances it is not surprising that the teachers found their own students pathetically passive. Professor McAulay reports that only 107 out of 1,909 teachers could say that their own youngsters initiated classroom discussions of controversial issues. At the same time, out of 1,898 teachers responding, 1,171, or 62 percent, declared that their children were definitely interested in controversial topics, their interest mostly stimulated by TV, parent discussion, magazine, radio, newspapers, and movies. (Only 41 teachers out of nearly 1,900 listed books as a source of stimulus.) Yet with so much latent concern and curiosity apparent to the teachers, they were either unwilling or unable to bring up in the classroom numerous issues and topics. What follows are the "controversial" *topics the teachers feel the children themselves are interested in* and why the teachers considered them taboo:

Number of teachers listing topics	Topics which teachers feel children might be interested in but which *the teachers* believe should not be discussed in their classroom
11	South Viet Nam
11	Homosexuals
13	Cuba

15	Local Politics
17	State Politics
26	Socialism
33	Sex
33	President Truman
35	Communism
41	Religion
52	Status of the Negro
61	China
63	Russia
65	Nuclear War
65	Teen-age Marriages
71	Atomic Testing
73	Gangsters
73	Corruption in Government
75	Disarmament
75	War with Russia
76	Divorce
81	Minority Groups
88	Family Quarrels
92	Desertion
101	Suicide

Number of teachers listing topics	Topics which the teachers believe the children are interested in but in which the *school administration* would feel a "deep concern" if they were discussed in class
83	Religion
91	Sex
106	Communism
183	Divorce
185	Family Problems
187	Extremist Groups

Number of teachers listing topics	Topics which the teachers thought interested their youngsters but in which *the community* would feel a "deep concern" if they were discussed in class
101	Labor Troubles
103	Integration
161	Politics
167	Disarmament
261	World Government
277	Family Problems
286	Civil Rights
301	Religion
491	Sex
486	Communism

The majority of teachers felt that their chief guardian of thought was the community itself. Out of 1,415 teachers, 1,154, or 82 percent, firmly believed that the taxpayers who supported the schools would not sanction the discussion of emotionally charged issues in the classroom.

This survey is instructive not only for what it suggests about the condition of American education but for what it may tell us about the reasons why schoolbooks ignore controversial issues or, if they present them, do so in a tepid fashion. (It takes some ingenuity for an American history textbook to ignore Senator Joseph McCarthy, but at least one current fifth-grade text manages to avoid the McCarthy era entirely).

By and large teachers are not known for their courage. They are quick to bow to what they believe are the desires of the community of non-educators who pay their salaries and put up the money for the purchase of the books they use to teach the community's children. Since the teachers

believe that the community which supports them dis-
approves of controversy, it is not surprising that the schoolbooks teachers approve and select avoid topics or issues
which might provoke thought among their students.

Moreover, many teachers have only a superficial knowledge of the subjects they do teach and thus their admission
of incompetence helps explain their satisfaction with the
books offered to them.* Finally, as previously suggested,
textbook publishers prefer to invest in those books which
promise the widest approval and sales and hence the biggest
profits. As a result they go to considerable lengths to ignore
ideas and issues which might disturb the placid, non-think
world of the community and the school.† Not surprisingly,
the schoolbooks which still offer the most outmoded view of
man and his world are the social studies texts, American and
world history books, and civics and problems-in-democracy
texts. Of necessity these books must attempt to deal with the
most sensitive areas of human thought and conflict.

While the social studies textbooks of the 1960's generally
fail to raise questions that might appear controversial, they
are also devoid of the overt racist theories of history which
permeated the schoolbooks of the nineteenth century. Where
today's textbooks err is not through commission but omission.
It is not that other peoples are portrayed as being racially
inferior. Rather, there is the repetitive, singsong refrain that
the United States, its allies, and the countries of its origin in
Western Europe represent most of what is good.

* One must add that more harm than good could result where a teacher
lacks the competence to handle controversial topics, particularly among
small children. One white teacher of an integrated second grade recently told a misbehaving Negro youngster that she wished he would go
back to where he came from. Fortunately the other children misinterpreted
her remark and asked how he could return to his mother's tummy. However,
it could prove appalling to have such a teacher deal with the subject of
integration.

† See Chapters 2, 4, 8, and 10 for discussions of controversial subjects
which have been deleted, ignored, or watered down by textbook publishers.

In 1966 the Lincoln Filene Center for Citizenship and Public Affairs at Tufts University published a preliminary report on twenty-four elementary social studies texts. Miss Astrid C. Anderson, the research assistant who wrote the report, notes that most grade-school social studies texts dwell on the theme that America got to be the way it is today because of the ax, hoe, gun, and plow, aided by thrift, endurance, and bravery in the face of overwhelming physical and natural odds. Those who brought this about invariably were the English, Spanish, French, and Dutch. Little or no mention is made of the crucial period of American history, the era of the greatest migration which led to the development of the cities. To view America this way, Miss Anderson writes, "is to exclude the Jew, the Greek, the Negro, the factory sweat-shop worker, the Cuban, the Irish, the Italian from getting 'equal time' in the elementary social studies book."

In "Racism in Geography," a paper prepared for the Department of Geography at Wayne State University, William Bunge summed up the simplistic, narrow view of today's schoolbooks. For children, he wrote, cannot help but "gain this strange historic-geographic dream that 'our' people were in Western Europe starting with the Renaissance. Before that 'our' people were in Rome building great roads. Before that 'our' people were in Greece, not as the dominant group of slaves, of course, but sitting around the temples calculating the shape and size of the earth. The Torch of Civilization just followed us about the map."

In the elementary grades the rest of the world is treated with the four-color vacuity of a Cook's travel brochure. Once a youngster has been educated in the platitudes of home and school in the first and second grades and has been imbued with the dynamics of the post office in the third grade, he travels in the fourth to faraway lands such as India where he discovers the Taj Mahal, curry, and bathing in the

Ganges, and Holland where he learns about tulips, red cheeses, and the virtue of Dutch cleanliness. As Miss Anderson observed, "The frequency with which these inoffensive, innocuous customs are associated with the high value placed in America on germ-free living should not go unnoticed."

By the time he has reached the fifth grade, the student is given the first of many year-long introductions to American history. Here ethnocentricity becomes the all-consuming point of view. A typical illustration of this view can be found in Harper & Row's *The Story of Our Country*. Like most fifth-grade histories, this text is pitched at a vocabulary level of the fourth grade so that the slow readers in the class will not feel left out. (Consider how stimulated you would feel if you could only read books which were purposely written beneath your intellectual capacity because the bottom third of library users were having trouble with *Ivanhoe*.)

In the chapter appropriately entitled "The United States Fought A Second World War," the authors of *The Story of Our Country* manage to attribute almost the entire Allied victory to America, with an occasional assist from England. The following passages which describe the military campaigns are found in a section entitled "Americans Fought to Victory."

Winning the Second World War required the best efforts of all Americans. More than twelve million men and women became members of the army, navy, marine corps, and coast guard. One army unit, which fought in Italy, was made up entirely of Japanese-Americans.

Citizens at home worked in factories that made war equipment for the nation. They gave up food so that there would be enough to feed the soldiers. Citizens at home were permitted to use only limited amounts of gasoline so that there would be fuel for tanks and airplanes. Americans everywhere made great sacrifices to achieve victory.

Following a two-paragraph description of how America won the Battle of the Atlantic, the child discovers:

Americans Fought in North Africa

The first important battles in which Americans took part were fought in North Africa, where German and Italian soldiers tried to capture Egypt. In 1942, an army made of American and British soldiers commanded by General Dwight D. Eisenhower landed in the western part of North Africa. At the same time, British troops stationed in Egypt attacked the enemy from the east. Finally, the Germans and Italians were defeated in North Africa.

Then the Americans and the British invaded Europe. First they captured Sicily, an island in the Mediterranean Sea near the coast of Italy. Then an attack was made on Italy itself.

In this section on how the war that engulfed the world was fought and won the words "American" and "United States" appear twenty-nine times, "British" eight, "Russians" three, "French" one, "Allies" one. In a previous passage there is one reference to China, and throughout there is no mention of Stalingrad, the entire European and Asian undergrounds, the troops of India, Australia, New Zealand, the Free French. It's as if Mighty Mouse had done it all.

Many current social studies and history books are also invested with an inflated sense of patriotism. Patriotic indoctrination begins with the entrance of the Founding Fathers who first appear in the fifth grade splendidly bedecked in periwigs and breeches, reappear in the eighth, again in the eleventh, and—if the youngster should attend college—once more in the sophomore year, where he will study American history for the fourth time. In "History in High-School Textbooks," an illuminating essay published in *School Review*, three historians, H. J. Noah, C. E. Prince, and C. R. Riggs, wrote: "Despite many studies of individual Fathers which cast doubt on the images of at least some of them as unselfish patriots, their unitary and common stereotypes have remained with remarkable persistence in the high-school textbooks. The Founding Fathers remain uniformly and without exception good and great men, disinterested promoters of the public welfare, sternly doing their duty to God and country."

The three scholars offer Robert Morris, "financier of the Revolution," as an extreme example of the distortions that take place. In portraying Morris textbook authors tend to revert to the antiquated versions of the nineteenth century and ignore twentieth-century historiography and scholarship. For instance, in the 1966 edition of Harcourt's *Rise of the American Nation,* the most popular American history text used in the eleventh grade, youngsters are taught the following:

> Robert Morris, a highly successful merchant and businessman of Philadelphia and a signer of the Declaration of Independence, handled the banking business for the Continental Congress. A man of great daring and far-ranging imagination, he resorted to many expedients to raise money for Washington's armies. Although the risks he took often brought him personally to the verge of bankruptcy, he never flagged in his efforts. It is questionable whether Washington's armies could have continued the struggle without the support that Robert Morris was able to provide.

No mention is made of the findings of such historians as Merill Jensen, whose work, *The New Nation, A History of the United States during the Confederation 1781–1789,* was published in 1950, or the writings of Thomas C. Cochran. Morris, according to these historians, was an avaricious businessman who possessed all the selfless virtues of a robber

baron. In *The New Nation* Jensen writes that it is a "myth
that Robert Morris financed the American Revolution, a
myth absurd if for no other reason than the fact that he did
not take office until the Revolution was virtually over.
Throughout the war he made money as an owner of priva-
teers and as an international merchant, selling goods at high
prices on both sides of the Atlantic. At the end of the Confederation . . . he still owed money to the United States.
Here commentary [of contemporary newspapers] coincided
with fact, for the books of the Treasury in 1790 showed him
to be the government's largest individual debtor." Jensen
goes on to note, "From 1782 to 1784, Morris the Superintendent [of Finance of the Confederation] borrowed a total of
about a million and a quarter dollars from Morris the
Banker." Morris also speculated wildly on western lands,
could not repay his fraudulent loans, and was sent to debtor's
prison in the 1790's.

Certainly more dangerous are the schoolbook accounts of
the Cold War, which impart a sort of *U. S. News and World
Report* version of history. Here the world is divided between
good guys (the West) and bad guys (communist countries).
Since McKinley, America has never committed any act
which may be questioned on moral grounds. Russia, on the
other hand, personifies evil and in the terrifying chess game
of the Cold War has never made a move which could be at
least partially explained as a legitimate, defensive ploy. With
only a few exceptions the typical high-school history text
feeds students numerous distortions. Consequently they are
not supplied with information that would permit them to
analyze today's events objectively.

The authors of "History in High-School Textbooks" report that in only one of the twelve schoolbooks they examined were they able to find an account that recognizes
that the Soviet Union is guided by historic Russian ambi-

tions as well as by Marxist dogma. "Other weaknesses follow from the original distortions," they add. "Although the mistakes, stupidities, and power-plays of the East are fully exposed, the mistakes, stupidities, and power-plays of the West tend to be omitted or played down."

To illustrate their point, the historians offer a comparison of the treatment given the U-2 incident and Castro's policies in Cuba. In D. C. Heath's *America, Land of Freedom,* high-school students are taught the following: "On May 1, shortly before the Paris Summit Conference, an American reconnaissance plane was shot down over Russia while photographing military bases without permission."

In an aside the authors of the *School Review* article admit they are puzzled by the phrase "without permission." Could the American U-2, they ask, have obtained permission by applying to the right Russian agency? They add, "Not merely is the language used the blandest possible, but the opportunity to explain the strengths and weaknesses of United States intelligence is not taken."

They then compare this bland, neutrally toned reference to a Western mistake with the language employed describing a country's shift to the left. In Ginn's *Our Country's History,* students are enlightened with the following interpretation of what took place in Cuba with the advent of Castro. "The red hand of communism," writes the author, David Muzzey, "was likewise seen at work in Cuba where dictator Castro broke with the Catholic Church, confiscated all American owned properties, and openly boasted of military aid from Russia and China."

What, ask the three historians, is one to make of the implication that breaking "with the Catholic Church" and confiscation "of all American owned properties" are clear evidence of Communist inspiration. Could it not be also said that these acts reflect nationalistic aspirations? And if this is one's interpretation, how does the historian—and student—view Martin Luther, Henry VIII, and George Washington? According to Muzzey's interpretation, they would have to be counted among the first Communists.

Certainly, the authors declare, better arguments for indicting Castro as a Communist could be offered. "Only the last of Muzzey's three reasons is valid in this context—a poor average for historical accuracy," they write. "One is driven to the conclusion that such passages use violence of language to gloss over deficiencies of careful thought and objectivity in presentation. As a result, students are not given sufficient information, objectively presented, to form valid bases for comparison between Western and Soviet methods."

There are many other examples. Four different textbooks describe Soviet intervention in Hungary but do not even mention the role played by the United States in intervention in Guatemala in 1954. In contrast to the treatment of Communist acts, much less attention is given to ignoble Western acts and policies, such as the Anglo-French attack on Egypt and Western support of reactionary leaders from Chiang Kai-shek and Salazar to Trujillo and Franco.

"The textbooks examined," the three historians declare, "leave the impression that Russian actions are sly, evilly motivated, and subversive, while Western moves represent honest, disinterested, and generous statesmanship. Nowhere is it even hinted at that responsible thinkers about the Cold War might hold the kind of view expressed by George F. Kennan in *Russia, the Atom and the West:* 'The Russians are not always wrong, any more than we are always right. Our task, in any case, is to make up our minds independently.' "

Even more dangerous is the American textbooks' interpretation of the rise of communism, which, write the three historians, the schoolbooks present as a conspiracy "moving by stealth, beards and bombs to accomplish its nefarious purposes." Rarely is the student given any hint of communism's great appeal. An exception is D. C. Heath's *The American Story,* which describes why Russian propaganda can prove effective. In this textbook it is pointed out that the underprivileged are told they are the victims of capitalist exploitation, that the personal liberties which democratic leaders talk about have no meaning for the poor, and that under communism all individuals will share land and housing without discrimination on the basis of race, color, or creed.

"In the great debate between the two systems which goes forward across the world today, and in which our students must participate," declare Noah, Prince, and Riggs, "textbooks leave them pitifully unwarned and unaware of the real strengths of communism. It is difficult to combat what one does not understand, and it is precisely this which, perhaps, constitutes the greatest danger in introducing propaganda into history textbooks."

That there are valid historical reasons for the United States to mistrust Russia and in turn sufficient cause for the Soviet Union to suspect American motives does not negate the fact that the attitudes of the American and Russian student, about to enter college, have been frozen by the doctrinaire education they have each received. The ultimate danger is not just a further polarization of the young who must inherit the Cold War, but the subversion of our own ideals and values.

"Because we in the West prize highly independent, critical thought in the attainment of truth," conclude Noah, Prince, and Riggs, "it is especially incumbent on us to make sure that our textbooks reflect this free tradition and do not distort history or invent historical 'facts.' It is a grave charge to make, but the conclusion is inescapable: under this treatment our students' minds tend to be closed, not widened. Students whose history reading is largely confined to the

textbook (and there are many such) are subjected to a brain-
washing as complete as it is dangerous. The burden placed
on the teacher is thus grievously enlarged, and he is hindered
in his task of enlightenment. The job of the teacher is not to
reinforce the making of myths, which the organs of mass
communications do only too well, but to acquaint the students with reality. In this high purpose, the high-school
history textbooks, in the fields [the Revolutionary War, Civil
War, and Cold War periods] that this paper has examined,
may be more of a hindrance than a help."

CHAPTER *8*

"Integration Is Not Castor Oil"

AMONG THE PERVERSIONS committed in the name of education, few equal the schoolbook's treatment of the Negro and his history. For more than 150 years he was presented to millions of children, both black and white, as a sub-human, incapable of achieving culture, happy in servitude, a passive outsider in the development and struggles of the American people. Such omissions of fact and commissions of error and falsehood continued throughout most of our own history as a democracy. Until the 1960's the American youngster saw an almost completely white world in the textbooks he studied. No Negro child ever romped with Spot, no Negro child ever performed a scientific experiment, no Negro child was ever portrayed as reading a book, hitting a baseball, playing a musical instrument.

As the student continued his education, he would most likely fail to find a schoolbook that mentioned the 5,000 Negro troops who fought in the American Revolution, the 168,000 Negro soldiers who joined the Union Army and who took part in 450 battles, the 30,000 Negroes who joined the Union Navy, the fourteen Negro Congressional Medal of Honor winners who received this country's highest award in the Civil War. Nor would he learn about the suffering of the slaves as they were transported to American shores, the numerous slave rebellions, the approximately 75,000 Negroes who escaped to freedom during the ten-year period before the Civil War, the honest Negro legislators who helped pass many good laws in the South during the Reconstruction Era, the two Negroes who served in the U. S. Senate between 1869 and 1901. Nor did the textbooks tell him about Benjamin Banneker, a brilliant Negro astronomer and mathematician who built the first clock ever made in America in 1753, the Negro abolitionist David Walker, whose book *Appeal* was published in 1829 and preceded Harriet Beecher Stowe's description of slavery by several decades, or Dr. Charles Drew, a leading researcher in blood plasma.

Instead of discovering the Negro's historic fight for freedom and his contribution to American culture in music and poetry, the student was presented with brief mention of Crispus Attucks, Booker T. Washington, George Washington Carver and, if the publisher was possessed of sufficient courage, Ralph Bunche. In this way the schools and the textbooks not only deprived the Negro child of a sense of his own worth and dignity but robbed the white child of any understanding of the Negro's own history. Indeed, it may be said that both white and Negro youngsters had been exposed to a form of racism in America more damaging than apartheid. In South Africa at least the whites recognize the physical existence of the blacks. In the American textbook the Negro's heritage, even the color of his skin, did not exist. In what has been described as an act of genius, the textbook industry managed to consign to oblivion one-tenth of the nation it sought to educate.

Then in the 1960's, nearly a hundred years after the Emancipation Proclamation, textbook publishers began putting the Negro into the schoolbooks. Not only did black children romp with Dick and Jane, but they and their parents joined their white counterparts in many of the normal activities that Americans, including Negroes, have been participating in for generations. Even more significant, the Negro's contribution to American history was being recognized so that he no longer appeared as the happy, dancing slave who had emancipation thrust upon him.

In the beginning these changes did not come about because the textbook publishers suddenly bore witness to their own conscience, although subsequently several have taken considerable financial risks by providing a full portrait of the Negro. Nor did the schools themselves publicly admit that they had been buying books which distorted or ignored the historical background of half their students. Rather, the driving force behind this change was the Negro Revolution itself, which opened the schoolbook market by forcing the big city Boards of Education and school systems to demand integrated textbooks. Indeed, the very process that brought the Negro and his history into the schools is not without interest. The Negro Revolution which first flowered in the streets of Montgomery and eventually marched into the North received a major impetus in the historic Supreme Court decision of 1954. The purpose of that ruling was to end school segregation, and, of course, it said nothing about integrating textbooks. However, because of the indirect support the Court's decision gave to the Negro Revolution, the Supreme Court's greatest contribution to education may not be school integration, which is still a long way from achievement, but the integration of the Negro into the American schoolbook, thus for the first time bringing him and his history into the classroom.

A telling illustration of the changes that have been made and the reasons they came about can be found by turning to the city of Detroit and an eighth-grade American history book published by Laidlaw Brothers, a textbook company in River Forest, Illinois.

Like most northern and western cities, Detroit's Negro population has markedly increased and now makes up more than 50 percent of the city's student body. While the education in Detroit's schools is not without its failings, the city does possess a fairly progressive urban school system. Yet here in the year 1962 eighth graders were still studying a textbook which contained passages that would have warmed the heart of the Grand Wizard of the Ku Klux Klan.* The book was entitled *Our United States: A Bulwark of Freedom.* At the time it was the only eighth-grade American history textbook that had been adopted by the Detroit Board of Education. It had also been selected by hundreds of other cities, including New York and Birmingham, Alabama.

In the 1961 version, then in use in the schools of Detroit, the three authors (one from the East, another from the Midwest, and the third representing the West) dealt with the subject of the slave owner and the effect "The War Between the States" had on the Negro by offering a fictitious account of a white family called the Austins, who lived on a large plantation about thirty miles from Nashville. The Austins, the authors explained, made their living from farming, although they never did any of the work themselves. Instead, Negro slaves planted and harvested the crops. "A white overseer, or hired hand," they wrote, "saw to it that the work was done properly."

Let us now join a thirteen-year-old Negro student in Detroit in 1962 as he returns to Idlewild, the Austin plantation in 1863:

---

* While the usual southern explanation is given for the origin of the KKK, this version does offer the fillip that the Klan did "terrible things" during Reconstruction.

(Henry Austin is interrupted by the sound of horses and a shriek from Cicero, a young slave. Cicero cries out, "Master Henry! The Yankees are coming." A squad of soldiers headed by a young United States lieutenant arrives on the scene and accuses Mrs. Austin of having concealed Confederate soldiers in her home. When she tells him such information is none of his business, the lieutenant informs her she has ten minutes to clear the valuables from her house before his soldiers burn it.)

A Proclamation Is Read. The Austins and their house slaves carried out the few valuables they still possessed and some of their fine furniture. Around the corner came the other slaves—women, children, old folks, and a few young men—herded along by the squad of soldiers. The children were crying as they clung fearfully to their mothers. When the slaves caught sight of Mrs. Austin, they broke away from the soldiers, came to her, and crouched behind her as though asking her for protection.

(The young lieutenant then mounts his horse and proceeds to read the Emancipation Proclamation which forever frees all slaves in states which were at war with the United States.)

When he had finished reaching the Presidential order, the lieutenant folded the paper and placed it inside his tunic. To his surprise the Austin slaves showed no joy over their freedom. They stood still, eyeing the soldiers suspiciously. Finally old Uncle Josephus stepped timidly forward.

"Please, sir," he said, cap in hand, "may we please go back to our work now?"

"Drat it, man!" the lieutenant lost his patience. "Didn't you understand what I've just said? You're free! You can do anything you want, go anywhere you want!"

"Lieutenant," Mrs. Austin raised her hand, "they don't understand what you have just read. We've kept them pretty much in ignorance of what has been going on, and, I'm afraid, we haven't done anything to make them trust you. May I talk to them?"

"Go ahead, Ma'am."

"Uncle Josephus," Mrs. Austin explained, "this lieutenant is your friend. What he means is that you no longer belong to us. The new law says that we can't keep you unless you want to stay. Those of you who wish to leave are free to do so; those of you who wish to stay in Idlewild are welcome. I can't pay you for working, but together we may be able to grow enough food to see us through."

"Sergeant!" the lieutenant called when Mrs. Austin was through speaking.

The sergeant gave a signal and the soldiers went about their task. Slowly, at first, the flames crept up to the white walls, licking hungrily at the paint. Within a few minutes the whole building was a mass of flames. The Austins turned away and clung to each other.

The textbook then asks this question:

How did the people on the plantation probably react to the burning of Idlewild?

To be sure, not well. But how did the Negro student in Detroit feel when he read about Uncle Josephus, the original Uncle Tom? Or when he read a one-sided debate between Mr. Austin, the defiant defender of slavery, and Allan Wright, one of his son's Harvard classmates who presents the anti-slavery view and who emerges as the cause's least promising advocate.

As it turned out, more than one Detroit family wondered how a progressive northern school system, half of whose students were Negro, could countenance a textbook which would have made excellent bedside reading in the ante-bellum South? Actually similar questions had been raised several times in the past. The biased treatment of the Negro in most schoolbooks had been pointed out in studies made by the American Council of Education in 1949, again by the Anti-Defamation League in 1961, and by a committee of eminent historians from the University of California, Berke-ley.* Although these reports had been widely publicized and read by both school administrators and textbook publishers, few had been concerned about changing the generally ac-cepted treatment of the Negro. While some school adminis-trators in Detroit had been troubled for a number of years by the schoolbooks' portrait of the Negro, no one had insisted upon changes in the textbooks.

Then in the fall of 1962 the local branch of the National Association for the Advancement of Colored People asked the Detroit Board of Education to withdraw immediately *Our United States* from the school system. In making its request the NAACP also presented a devastating critique of the book. It was joined in its protest by Richard B. Henry, a Negro leader and president of the Group on Advanced Leadership, who gained additional newspaper publicity by keeping his son, Frederick, out of history class.

"As far back as 1952 we were concerned about the treat-ment of minorities in the textbooks," said Dr. Elmer F. Pflieger, divisional director of social studies in Detroit. "But we were just so many voices in the wilderness. Then came the revolution in the 1960's which forced the textbook pub-lishers to pay attention and Detroit to act."

The time was indeed ripe. The Board of Education set up a special committee to examine the text it had already adopted. The committee finally concluded that the com-

---

* The Berkeley report was unanimously accepted by the California State Board of Education on March 12, 1964.

plaints were justified. The Board then took two steps. In an interim move it ordered its educators to write a supplementary booklet which would be used along with the history textbook. The booklet which was written in about four months corrected the abuses in *Our United States* and was then shipped out to the schools where it was studied in conjunction with the textbook in question, thus unwittingly providing a fascinating lesson in the art of historiography. At the same time the Board advised publishers that teaching materials must "contribute significantly to understanding and good will among different racial, religious and minority groups."

Finally, in November, 1963, about one year after the NAACP's original protest, the Board took an even more drastic step. It ordered the discontinuance of *Our United States* and called for the selection of a replacement. In effect the Board of Education was telling the textbook industry it could no longer cater to the viewpoint of much of the southern market and still hope to sell its textbooks in Detroit. Dr. Carl Byerly, assistant superintendent for the improvement of instruction, recalled the effect his system's edict had on some members of the industry: "One of the publishers said, 'If we win an adoption in Detroit, we don't care about Mississippi. We sell more books in Detroit.'"

While *Our United States* was making headlines in the city's newspapers and gaining attention in the editorial columns, Laidlaw Brothers, the schoolbook's publisher, was busy revising its rejected version. Not only did the publisher remove the objectionable Austin family, but it incorporated most of the information contained in "The Struggle for Freedom and Rights," the pamphlet which the schools' specialists had written. "We had wondered how the author [of *Our United States*] had shifted and changed so quickly," Dr.

Pflieger remarked. "Then we noticed in the revised book that they had added a consultant."

Of the dozen eighth-grade history books submitted, the Detroit selection committee adopted the revised edition of *Our United States*. It is this new version that eighth-grade students have been using since September, 1964.

In an article published in "Teachers College Record," Dr. Sol M. Elkin, a sociologist at Wayne State University in Detroit, posed the question: Why, despite the effort to insure a wise choice, and despite the selection of a book that is substantially similar to previously acceptable books, did *Our United States* become a target of this unprecedented barrage of criticism?

"The explanation," he wrote, "lies in the increasing pace and intensity of the Negro's assault on the barriers that block his full participation in the life of 'our United States.' Pressure to revise this text can be viewed as a part of the greater protest. The disputed textbook, like other alleged discriminations, is not really new; neither is its unacceptability to Negroes. Only now, however, resentment at the negative image of the Negro in school textbooks has found organized expression."

In part because of organized Negro protests and the subsequent pressures brought to bear on publishers by Detroit, New York City, Pittsburgh, Los Angeles, there have been improvements in the treatment of the Negro in junior- and senior-high-school history texts. In "The Negro in Modern American History Textbooks," * a study of five junior-high

* This study was underwritten and published in October, 1966, by the American Federation of Teachers. Sloan, a forty-year-old graduate of Harvard Law School, notes that he is neither primarily a historian or scholar. He is a teacher who has been studying and teaching Negro history for several years. For this reason, he says in his introductory remarks, he used the criteria set out in the University of California report to judge the history texts he examined.

and eight high-school texts frequently used in the schools, Irving Sloan, a social studies teacher in Scarsdale, New York, and the author of the study was able to note, "One need go back only to the 1950s and compare those editions with 1966 editions of the same texts to see the startling changes and improvements."

Nevertheless Sloan was moved to comment that even the "best" accounts leave room for further improvement. He then goes on to mention some of the "shocking" distortions or omissions still found in many of the current editions. "For example," he reports, "the treatment of the rise of the Ku Klux Klan as a response to the Reconstruction governments in almost all of the texts implies a moral justification, suggesting that the 'moderate whites' had no choice. Rarely is there an expression of disapproval of the activities of the Klan."

Here follows some of Sloan's other findings in his survey of the thirteen American history books studied by most of the nation's junior- and senior-high-school students:

1. That the Negroes who first arrived in English America came as indentured servants, not as slaves. This at least suggests to the student that it was not an inherent racial inferiority which explains why Negroes became slaves. Unfortunately, only one text indicates that the first Negroes were here with the Spanish explorers, so that their presence in America precedes the English colonists.
2. That slavery as an institution was degrading to masters and slaves alike. A few of the texts, however, still cling to the romanticized versions of the happy slave life.
3. That the abolition movement was not just a white movement. No text gives enough attention to the participation of Negroes in this struggle for freedom.
4. That Negroes made significant contributions to the wars fought by the United States. While most texts mention the fall of Crispus Attucks in the Boston Massacre, and the num-

ber of Negroes who fought in the Civil War, rarely do any of them give this adequate discussion.

5. That between Reconstruction and the 1954 Supreme Court decision, the American Negro did not "disappear." In analysis after analysis of the texts, the reader will find the statement that after Reconstruction "200–300 pages pass before we get a reference to the Negro." This is why whites do not always "see" Negroes. As Ralph Ellison puts it, they are "invisible." And the reason they are unseen is that they are left out from such a large part of American history. In most of the texts it can be said that the Negro is considered only as a slave before the Civil War and a problem since the Civil War.

6. That the Civil Rights movement should not be explained only in the light of this 1954 decision and the 1964 Civil Rights Act. Very few of the texts included in this study trace the economic, social, and political abuses endured by the Negro in both the North and the South through the long years of his "emancipation."

As Irving Sloan notes, this last generalization and others match the conclusions drawn by Miss Astrid C. Anderson in her report on elementary-school social studies texts conducted at the behest of the Lincoln Filene Center for Citizenship and Public Affairs. (See Chapter 7.) Sloan writes, "In that part of her survey dealing with the treatment of the American Negro in elementary school texts, Miss Anderson shows a far worse and therefore more deplorable situation than that in the secondary school texts. Elementary school students, after all, are in their most formative years and the need for historical truth and perspective is at least as vital as it is in the upper grades. On the whole, the grade school history texts are insipid, inadequate, and inaccurate."

Where one can find marked improvement in the grade-school texts is in the illustrations. For it is in these texts, more profusely illustrated than the junior- and senior-high-school books, that the black child and adult have at last become visible. The extent of the change can be seen in a survey conducted by the NAACP in the summer of 1966, which found integrated illustrations in 175 pre-school and elementary classroom texts. And as the survey noted, the list was not complete. Nearly all the editions mentioned had been published between 1962 and 1966. Prior to 1962 only a handful of elementary schoolbooks contained a dark face.

These improvements, however, did not always come about just because publishers finally decided to color some of the white children brown. The problem and issues can be more complex than that.

One of the first textbook publishers to issue integrated schoolbooks was Follet Publishing Company in Chicago. In 1953 Follet published *Big City Fun,* a social studies text for the third and fourth grade, which contained integrated illustrations of Negroes and whites. Then in 1959 Follet put out an integrated social studies series for grade schools, while continuing to sell its all-white edition.

"Even New York was not asking for the integrated text then," said Bob Follet, the young general manager of the firm's Educational Division. "Nor was there an overwhelming demand in the suburban areas except for those communities heavily populated with liberal Jewish people. You know, I have the feeling we'll be selling our integrated books in Atlanta and Dade County before we sell them in some of our lily-white suburbs."

Follet and a number of leading publishers had joined fourteen major cities in the Great Cities Project, an attempt to improve the education of the culturally deprived. In keeping with this program Detroit had shown interest in obtaining simple integrated basic readers which would reflect the life of the city. The Detroit school system offered to write the books but also insisted upon final approval of content and illustrations. Follet agreed to Detroit's terms and brought out the first experimental edition in 1961.

"We had to destroy ten thousand books," Bob Follet recalled. "Although there was no garbage in the streets, we had a scene showing a line of brownstones with the children playing on the stoop and the sidewalk. These were obviously inner-city dwellings. The family had no visible father and he did not play any part in the story. Detroit had found that fifty percent of the culturally deprived had no father.

"The Negro press responded vigorously," Bob Follet continued. "They were protesting against the implication that an integrated community exists only in the slums. They also were protesting against the implied social propaganda that would make the Negro satisfied with his downtrodden lot. So the decision was made to show aspirations instead of reality."

In the revised series the Negro and white families live in salt-box frame houses located in a lower-middle-class suburb. The doghouse built for Wiggles is made out of wooden shingles and the swimming pool consists of inflatable plastic. The first character to appear is "Father." One of the typical decisions that had to be made was whether "Father" should be portrayed as a white-collar worker wearing a tie and a white shirt or as a blue-collar worker carrying a lunch pail. It was finally decided he should come striding home in a brown shirt and blue jacket, carrying a *newspaper*.

"We had an extremely difficult time finding an artist," Bob Follet said. "There were some Negro artists we found who had never drawn a Negro face or who were afraid that criticism would arise on how they drew Negroes."

Ruth Ives, the artist eventually chosen, solved the problem by simply drawing a handsome family that are undeniably Negro.

In a study of three of the pre-primers, conducted by the Detroit school system, which it must be noted also created the books, the question was raised: How does the substitution of Negro and white characters for the typical all-white characters affect children?

"As shown earlier," the report concluded, "first-grade children are generally not race conscious. According to the reports of teachers, the children made no mention of the fact that the group of playmates appearing in the City Schools books is racially mixed. In all classes, Caucasian, Mixed, and Negro, the children manifested a marked preference for the City Schools Series. When asked individually to indicate the child character they preferred as schoolmate and playmate, the children gave highest rank to the Negro characters of the City Schools Series. Nevertheless every evidence indicated that the choices were not made on the basis of race. Instead, the children were intrigued by the realistic stories featuring exciting adventures such as they themselves might have."

While taking an important step forward in integrating grade-school books, a number of publishers have simultaneously perpetuated segregated education by continuing to sell all-white or what one editor called "mint julep" editions of the same books. For example, Scott, Foresman, the nation's largest elementary-school publisher, is still selling integrated and all-white editions of their grade-school social studies, health and reading series.* In the integrated readers apple-cheeked, blond Jane and Sally and their brother Dick play with three Negro children, Penny, Pam, and Mike. In the segregated edition all the children are white.

* Under the law or by contractual arrangement, the publisher in some states or communities is obligated to supply copies of specific editions previously adopted. This means that for several years to come the publisher must continue to provide the older, all-white edition to some schools or states. However, while Scott, Foresman is not obligated by law or contract to sell its older all-while edition in new adoption situations, it continues to do so where the adopting authorities indicate a preference for it.

However, these are not the only differences. Chicago's fourth graders, who use the integrated Scott, Foresman reader, learn about Benjamin Banneker, the Negro astronomer, while youngsters in the same grade in the South and many northern communities read instead about Paul Revere. In the integrated sixth-grade reader children learn about the African slave trade and how a Negro boy saves a white playmate from drowning. In the "mint julep" edition both stories are omitted.

Despite the fact that a number of major publishers plan to continue to sell two separate editions, every editor and sales executive I interviewed on the subject agreed that minority children get a feeling of inferiority when the only youngsters they see in the books are white. How then could publishers justify plans to continue to print and sell segregated schoolbooks?

Kenneth Lund, a senior vice-president and editor in chief, said, "We continue to serve our existing customers who want all-white texts and those adopting customers who want new materials. Educational policy does not rest with us. It is made by the states, local school boards, administrators, and teaching staffs. We produce for them the kinds of materials they want. In our business the customer chooses."

At least three large publishers, however, have agreed to give up the lucrative southern market if textbook selection committees insist on all-white texts. Frank Paparello, executive science editor at Holt, Rinehart and Winston in New York, recently asked five authors of a new elementary science series whether they wanted one or two editions. "Three of the authors," Paparello recalled, "wanted dual editions. They said that they had put in an awful lot of work and that we would lose a lot of business in the South. The other two authors voted for just an integrated edition even if we should lose the southern business." Despite the preference of the majority of authors, Holt will publish only one edition and it will be integrated. So will Harcourt, Brace & World and Silver Burdett in their forthcoming textbooks. "It simply comes down to what you believe," Frank Paparello said.*

So far two southern states, Virginia and Louisiana, have adopted integrated texts, according to Craig Senft, president of Silver Burdett.† For Louisiana this action represents a marked change in policy. 'The first question the chairman of the Louisiana textbook selection committee used to ask was: 'You got any niggers in your book?' " Senft said. "The publishers representative would say, 'No, sir.' Two years ago we decided we would not produce one series for Detroit and New York and another for the South. Some of our friends said, 'You are absolutely crazy. You'll ruin the company.' Our really difficult decision was whether we should submit integrated texts in states like Louisiana. We did, and in December, 1965, Louisiana adopted both our integrated music and science series."

In addition to integrating illustrations, some publishers are willingly making other changes which could endanger sales. "For instance, when we revised *Rise of the American Nation*," said Harcourt editor Donald Stewart, "we made it clear that after the federal government left the South and the whites took over, this led to Jim Crow and discrimination. We also included a final chapter on the course of Negro civil rights developments."

This version of Harcourt's eleventh-grade American history was published at the start of 1966, but the decision to

* It should be noted that generally those publishers who are issuing only integrated editions are doing so with new series in subject areas they have not previously covered. The publishers with heavy investments in all-white editions are continuing to publish those editions plus the integrated editions.

† In the spring of 1967, Scott, Foresman reported that it had some success in getting its Open Highways Series, which is offered only in a multi-ethnic edition, adopted in Mississippi. This series of readers is used to teach reading to slow learners.

revise it was made four years earlier. "The civil rights revolution had gained in intensity," Stewart recalled, "and Bill Jovanovich said to the authors and me, 'You do what you believe to be right.' We made the changes and Jovanovich then okayed them.

"This is a very valuable piece of property," he added. "Our sales of this one book run around one million dollars and two hundred thousand copies a year. When we did make the changes we knew we might lose the South and this could cost us one-fourth of our sales."

Without minimizing the responsibility of textbook publishers and the nation's school systems, it must be noted that the problem of integrating the Negro in schoolbooks is not without frustrations. Shortly after the Detroit Board of Education sent out a directive calling for the selection of instructional materials that reflected "fair treatment for all groups in our society," the administration decided to adopt a new Latin textbook.

"The selection committee finally picked one," recalled Dr. Carl Byerly, an assistant superintendent. "Then a Negro member of the committee said that there was no picture of a Negro in the textbook. It did not reflect the American way of life. You know, she went on, a Latin book could reflect Negro civilization in Africa. The Romans, she said, knew about that. I told her I am not convinced the Romans knew all about that. And besides, she was talking about history, not Latin."

The protesting member of the selection committee threatened to bring the problem to the Board of Education if she did not get her way. The superintendent of Detroit's schools resolved the dispute by rejecting all the new Latin texts. He then ordered the Latin teachers to continue with the textbook already in use.

"This committee member's complaint reflected the vocal

Negro groups whom she had gotten behind her," Dr. Byerly added. "A year or so later we adopted a new Latin text without integrated illustrations."

There is also a danger that some publishers in an attempt to cater to the "integrated school market" will provide a distorted view of history. An illustration of what can happen was reported by Fred Hechinger, education editor of *The New York Times*. In 1956 Noble and Noble published *New York Past and Present*, a history of New York which was still in use in some of the city's fourth grades as late as November, 1966. Incredibly, this schoolbook, which mentions almost every member of the great melting pot, never refers to Negroes except as "darkskinned natives" whose pictures appear in a chapter on "How People Live on a Tropical Island." There is an additional chapter on the Lapps, which may suggest that the authors also had a problem with geography.

Ten years later, Hechinger notes, Noble and Noble issued *The New York Story*, an equally curious document. After the student has absorbed the chapter on Presidents from New York State, he proceeds to read the following chapters: "Outstanding Negroes," "Famous Negro Athletes," "Well-Known Negro Singers and Entertainers," "Negro Poets and Authors," and "Other Well-Known Negroes." All this is followed by two chapters on Puerto Ricans and then two paragraphs which mention all the other minority groups.

It is the responsibility of publishers to put on the printed page "what people ought to know, not just what will sell," declared Whitney Young, Jr., in a speech before the American Textbook Publishers Institute. The executive director of the National Urban League added, "Don't approach integration like castor oil. For once, look at something not as a problem but as an opportunity."

The way to avoid treating a person as a human being, he

continued, is to fail to report his accomplishments and instead to foster types like Little Black Sambo and Amos and Andy. "No one," he added, "is going to hire Amos as a chemist."

At the same time he noted that while the Negro's history is ignored, there is also a tendency to give the Negro too much credit for originality. "The participants in the Boston Tea Party (as is well reported in your textbooks) and not James Farmer invented civil disobedience in this country," he declared. "Susan B. Anthony and the suffragettes started demonstrations in the streets. The labor movement started sit-ins. We didn't invent block voting; how did Mayor Curley in Boston get re-elected time and time again? The Negro is in the best tradition of America; he has learned well, from the textbook publishers of America."

The problem, however, of reaching inner-city children, more than half of whom are Negro and most of whom come from depressed homes, is not solved just by integrating texts and recognizing the Negro contribution to American history. To stimulate both white and black youngsters who have been bred in the ghettos or slums, schoolbooks must portray a reality that is meaningful to them. This means that traditional works like *Silas Marner* and *Ivanhoe* are no longer appropriate for school study for thousands of children. At the same time it does not follow that urban youngsters should be deprived of "culture" simply because many of them come from "culturally deprived" homes. Rather they must first be taught to read and then be stimulated by the right reading material before they can attempt to absorb and enjoy some of the complexities of Milton or Goethe.

It is to the credit of several schoolbook publishers that they are now attempting to reach the deprived youngster by issuing graded literature texts which contain material that on occasion is both starkly realistic and of high enough quality to be worthy of a child's learning time. In doing so they are getting out of the rut of "mass culture education" by taking into account group differences and interests.

As with almost every other advance in textbook publishing, the issuance of such schoolbooks only became possible when the taboos against realistic material were lifted. "Sherwood Anderson's 'Brother Death' took ten years to get into a ninth-grade anthology," recalled Leo Kneer, the general editor of Scott, Foresman's junior- and senior-high-school English texts. "It was the opposition of other editors and authors to the idea of the 'pretty school.' If we think children do not think about death, we're wrong. It intrigues them."

As Leo Kneer himself would readily note, not all the taboos have disappeared. On occasion the problem of realism combines with the problem of integration to pose what appears to be an insuperable dilemma.

Not long ago Scott, Foresman issued a new American literary anthology for eleventh-grade students. Entitled *Accent: U.S.A.*, this schoolbook contains *Thunder on Sycamore Street*, a TV drama by Reginald Rose. At the end of the selection the editors appended two notes. The first note explains to the student that, like the central character in Rose's drama, the Younger family in Lorraine Hansberry's *A Raisin in the Sun* believes it has the right to live in any neighborhood it selects. "But the Youngers are Negroes," the schoolbook says, "and the people of Clybourne Park say they have worked hard to build their community and want to live only near people who share a common background."

The second note explains the origin of Rose's TV drama and some of the problems the author faced in getting it produced:

> *Thunder on Sycamore Street* was originally presented on "Studio One." Reginald Rose says that it was written as a direct

result of a 1954 newspaper article which had to do with race riots at a housing development in a suburb of Chicago. The main character of the play was planned as a Negro, but at that time, Rose says, it would have been impossible to get network approval, so he made him an ex-convict instead.* Rose feels that the character thus became more universal because the play was interpreted in many ways by many groups.

What the student is not told is that the literature department of Scott, Foresman had originally considered publishing *A Raisin in the Sun* in its new eleventh-grade anthology. However, the play was rejected, mainly because, in the first act, the young mother, Ruth, seeks an abortion. It was felt, too, that it would not seem probable for one of the characters to attend college while coming from a lower-class, non-intellectual home.

"It was my decision not to use the play," said Leo Kneer. "I was also afraid of the whispered comments that might come from Negro or white students, like, 'I don't want them living near me.' It could turn the class into chaos."

Thus *A Raisin in the Sun* was kept out of a schoolbook partly for the same reason that Reginald Rose rewrote *Thunder on Sycamore Street*, to avoid the direct portrayal of the realistic and controversial issue of suburban white prejudice against Negroes. Since Rose wrote his original drama over a decade ago television has apparently matured. During the Christmas season of 1966 CBS dealt with this very theme by presenting the movie based on Lorraine Hansberry's play. The question remains: how many years must pass before a schoolbook will do the same?

* The ex-convict also happens to be white.

CHAPTER *9*

Up From McGuffey

EARLY ONE MORNING in 1841 a young man by the name of Winthrop B. Smith climbed the stairs to a small second-floor office on Cincinnati's Main Street. Smith, whose austere appearance was enhanced by full, bushy eyebrows and a broad forehead, had come to sever in two the publishing firm of Truman & Smith, which William B. Truman and Smith himself had founded seven years earlier. While Smith waited for his partner to arrive at their office, he proceeded to make a pile of the firm's miscellaneous books which included their first copyrighted work, *The Child's Bible with Plates* by "a lady of Cincinnati," and a collection of church music entitled *Mason's Sacred Harp*. On top of this collection Smith put all the firm's cash. He then made a second, smaller pile of schoolbooks.

Finally Truman appeared, only to be informed by Smith that their partnership had come to an end. Smith then asked Truman to choose either the cash and the miscellaneous books or the smaller collection of textbooks. As legend has it, Truman pounced upon the money and works under it and thereby committed one of publishing's historic blunders. For the books he had rejected included early editions of

McGuffey's Eclectic Readers, which were to become one of the most popular series of textbooks published in America. From 1836 to 1900 half the schoolchildren in the nation read McGuffey, whose sales eventually totaled nearly 125 million copies. Of *Mason's Sacred Harp* there is only a history of oblivion.

Not surprisingly, a few commentators have been concerned with the publishing history of McGuffey. Rather their interest has centered around the Readers' influence on the tastes and values of a maturing nation. It is easy to see why. The series of six books which were continually revised over the years not only taught youngsters how to read, but the more difficult volumes provided most of the literature to which three generations of Americans were exposed. In the sixth and final Reader youngsters of about fifteen were presented with excerpts from such literary luminaries as Shakespeare, Samuel Johnson, Dryden, Addison, Milton, Goldsmith, Macaulay, Longfellow, Poe, and Horace Greeley. Along with this acquaintance with culture the Readers, through fable and story, taught morals and good sense. Even the Primer and First Reader, which contained words usually no longer than one syllable, exhorted the young to eschew idleness and sloth. "Mary was up at six," intoned the Primer. "Up, up, Lucy, and go out to Mary!" Scoffers, wrote Mark Sullivan, abbreviated that to "Double up, Lucy!" Most people, however, did not scoff. Rather, men like Teddy Roosevelt and Henry Ford and thousands of others whose intellect was honed by McGuffey looked back on the education they received from those schoolbooks with awe and nostalgia.

However, that aspect of McGuffey which may interest us now is the effect the Readers had on textbook publishing. For the McGuffey Readers were among the first schoolbooks to reflect modern-day publishing methods. Not only did

Truman and Smith employ salesmen who visited schools, but they pioneered the practice of having schoolbooks written to order. Moreover, as it has happened to many present-day textbooks, the McGuffey Readers were to take on a life of their own during which the original author at first approved revisions made by others and eventually had his place taken by editors who brought the books up to date.

Also like the textbook houses of the mid-1960's, Truman and Smith were to benefit from two almost concurrent boons: a population explosion and an outpouring from the Federal Treasury. Cincinnati, where the young men began their publishing venture in 1834, was the focal point of western business, and the West was experiencing considerable economic and population expansion. Two years later when the McGuffey Readers began to make their appearance the Federal Treasury had, of all things, a surplus which was turned over to the states, sixteen of whom used the moneys to build schools and hire teachers. Although Truman and Smith had not actually anticipated this windfall, the McGuffey Readers were soon to fill the demands of a fast-growing market.

Even before the size of this market was apparent, Winthrop Smith sought out an author to provide a series of textbooks whose content would reflect the mores of the period and region.

"The common schools of the new West," a historian wrote, "were non-sectarian—they were the outgrowth of the strong democratic belief in common-school education. Established by law, and supported by public money, they were free of the religious control that dominated the colonial schools. The very atmosphere of the Cincinnati home of the publisher made it logical for them to move away from the churchly influence. But no innovation can be too new: the strength of the ties to the past is too great, and though they moved into new paths, they looked back and kept their bearings by introducing a strong moral and ethical tone in their new readers. Even the new West believed in the unequivocal code of right and wrong—and the necessity of bringing up the young in the way they should go. . . ."

Winthrop Smith believed he knew just the educator who could write and compile the schoolbooks which would incorporate the ethics of the new West. Early in 1836 he called on Catherine Beecher, who, with her sister, was running a girls' school in Cincinnati. Miss Beecher turned down Smith's offer because of her involvement with the school. Had she accepted the young publisher's proposal she might have achieved greater fame than her sister Harriet, who later became the author of *Uncle Tom's Cabin*.

Instead, Catherine Beecher recommended William Holmes McGuffey, a licensed Presbyterian preacher and a teacher of mental philosophy at Miami University in Oxford, only thirty miles from Cincinnati. The son of an Indian fighter and scout, McGuffey was born near the western border of Pennsylvania in 1800. A few years later the family moved to Trumbull County, Ohio. The story, which was repeated for several generations, was that the McGuffeys were too poor to give their children a proper education. During the summer of 1818 a Presbyterian clergyman by the name of Thomas Hughes was riding through the backcountry of Trumbull County seeking funds for a school that he ran. As the minister passed a log cabin, half hidden by the bushes, he heard a woman praying aloud. She was asking God if He might somehow provide schooling for her youngsters. The clergyman rode on to the next cabin where he learned the family's name, returned, and took it upon himself to educate the oldest son, William McGuffey.

Like many of the fables McGuffey was to insert in his Readers, this story eventually proved a pleasant fiction. However, McGuffey did become a scholar of sorts and, it would

seem, in his later years, one of his most fervent admirers. It
has been said that during his lifetime he gave over three
thousand sermons and, if asked, could recall every word he
had ever preached. Though a failure as a school adminis-
trator and something of a windbag, McGuffey was to win
fame, if not his fortune, as a textbook author.

At Miss Beecher's behest, Smith approached McGuffey
who readily agreed to write and compile the Readers. He
also signed a contract which gave him a 10 percent royalty.
However, the agreement stipulated that as soon as McGuffey
received a total of $1,000, the schoolbooks were to become
the property of the publisher. Though McGuffey later
received an annuity, he never earned the fortune he could
have had had he not agreed to a limitation of earnings.
Commented historian Charles Carpenter, "Had McGuffey
made such contracts as did [Noah] Webster he probably
would have become one of the wealthy men of the country.
Such a result would have depended, of course, upon whether
the publishers would have pushed the books as hard as they
did, and had McGuffey continued to receive royalties."

No sooner had Truman and Smith launched the Readers
than they were faced with a pressing legal complication. In
1837 the publisher and the author of the most famous series
of schoolbooks extolling the virtues of rectitude were sued
for plagiarism. The suit was brought by the easern publishers
of the *Worcester Readers*, who claimed that McGuffey had
copied at least ten pieces from the Worcester series as well
as the scheme for the Third and Fourth McGuffey Readers.
On Christmas Day, 1838, a temporary Federal Court injunc-
tion was issued against the publication of the McGuffey
books. Winthrop Smith, however, had already expunged the
offending passages, substituting a total of seventeen new
selections, thus providing the first of many revisions of the
series. Once the changes were made Truman & Smith again

sold McGuffey to the schools. Two years later, as the result of a ruling made by a court-appointed referee, the owners of the *Eclectic Readers* paid $2,000 in damages to the publisher of the *Worcester Readers*.

It wasn't long before the McGuffey Readers began their phenomenal penetration of the western and southern markets. Within the next decade McGuffey was dominating a large section of American education. By the late 1880's, a half century after the first books appeared, the series was still selling at the rate of over two million copies a year. Over the years the books were continually revised by a variety of editors including Smith himself and the author's brother, Alexander H. McGuffey. Between 1836, when the McGuffey First Reader appeared, and 1890 the series passed through the corporate hands of seven different publishers, finally coming to rest under the imprint of the American Book Company which in 1966 sold 25,000 copies to the curious and nostalgic.

Up to this period there were a number of textbook publishers in both the East and the West who competed vigorously for the schoolbook market. Like their predecessor, Truman & Smith, they originated the books themselves, selected the authors, hired editors to make the necessary revisions, and then sold the texts through platoons of traveling salesmen. However, around 1890 there was a radical change in the structure of the textbook industry. For this was the era of the great trusts and the schoolbook publishers were no less immune to the chicanery and monopolistic practices of the times. The worst offender was McGuffey's last publisher, the American Book Company, which had gained control of between 75 and 80 percent of the nation's textbook business. As one troubled educator of that period observed, "Even the notorious Standard Oil Company has no such monopoly as this."

The American Book Company, which operated as a trust throughout the 1890's, employed all the techniques which so fascinated the muckrakers. In 1897, George A. Gates, president of Iowa College in Grinnell, delivered a scathing speech before the Iowa Teachers' Association describing the trust's methods. The paper, replete with affidavits, included in its catalogue of chicanery: bribery, cajolery, threats of loss of employment, securing the election or appointment of school officials and board members who would adopt the company's books, and the suborning of local newspapers.

Most of the bribes offered to schoolteachers, principals, and superintendents consisted of petty sums, often no more than $100, which either attests to the perennial problem of low salaries paid educators or the general human condition whereby he who pays a bribe often finds a man's honor is the cheapest commodity on the market.

For example, an American Book Company salesman in Iowa promised to provide an all-expense paid vacation "up the river to Duluth" for a school superindendent and his family if the official would persuade his Board of Education to adopt all of the firm's textbooks. In Illinois a representative of the trust offered to bribe a school-board member if he would vote against the adoption of a rival firm's geography textbook. "We do not want to expose ourselves to a trial for bribery, but I will give you a hundred dollars for that pen on your desk," the agent declared. One enraged city superintendent wrote George Gates, explaining why teachers and principals were so hesitant in offering information about the trust's selling methods.

"Allow me," he declared, "to suggest an explanation for the timidity of school principals. Many of them are effectually silenced by the premeditated policy of the publishers. These have made gifts of books, they have offered privileges for handling books, they have solicited correspondence, they have used all the wiles of the devil, until the unsuspecting school teacher has built up a line of suspicious evidence in the letter-books of the publisher which would destroy his influence if hurled down upon him in the midst of a book fight. I have known this from the inside for fifteen years, and yet some of my correspondence with book houses, if placed before the public with my enemies' interpretations, would not help me in time of a book fight. One who has not seen it from the other side can scarcely comprehend the deviltry with which a man is pursued by these book fiends who spare neither character nor honor in their greed for spoils."

Although a number of teachers and school officials refused to accept the book trust's blandishments and defied the agents when they attempted blackmail, many others accepted money or favors from the company. In one eastern state most of the county school supervisors were moonlighting as salesmen for the American Book Company, working in every community except their own, where their appearance as agents would have proved embarrassing. In Oregon a committee of forty-one educators was set up to select schoolbooks for the state for a period of six years. Of the texts chosen, 98 percent were published by the book trust. The chairman of a citizens' protest committee declared, "I am informed that twenty-one of the votes cast were almost duplicates, a somewhat remarkable thing, considering the fact that the voters did not meet and probably had hundreds if not thousands of textbooks to select from."

The gravest danger posed by the trust was that it had the power to determine what should be taught in American schools. This power stemmed from the fact that the trust not only published most of the books used in the schools but literally owned the allegiance of many of those school officials who were responsible for selecting them.

"Much might be made of the fact," Gates wrote, "that while American Book Company has on its list many valuable books written by the ablest authors, it is also true that their list contains some of the most disgraceful trash. They have many antiquated books. The general public of course cannot judge of this. But let the question be asked of intelligent teachers or any one familiar with the school book publications of the last quarter century. Now what does this firm do, especially in our frontier or 'back-woods' states, when it can secure by some of the methods mentioned above control of the school book trade, but put in these out-of-date books. Books that are referred to nowadays as a laughing stock by intelligent teachers are foisted upon whole states for a series of years. The agents know that the territory is completely in their power. It is monopoly in its most odious form."

The book trust, because its power was so great, was able to keep out of the classroom any subject, point of view, or innovation which its managers did not like. It was during this period that the book monopoly issued a new sociology text for high-school and college students. And how, George Gates asked, was the general subject of the trusts themselves treated in the American Book Company's new textbook? "In this book of nearly four hundred pages," he wrote, "just eleven lines, in three different places, are given to the whole subject of trust, combinations and monopolies. In each place they are defended and excused."

Or consider the problem of the teacher who sought an improved geography textbook. For years the American Book Company published all the geographies used in the schools. Thus no new geographies were issued until one of the few remaining firms finally dared to take on its nearly monolithic competitor and publish what Gates described as "an admirable book" on the subject. "The result," he added, "is that there is a fight all along the line. The teachers set up a clamor for a change, the matter is laid before the city and county school boards with whom the decision lies. The book men get information of the discussion and rush to the field. Then begins the old story of bribes and promises and threats by the American Book Company's agents to secure the retention of the old books. My point here is that the only hope for improved text-books in geography has been the fact that the monopoly power is not quite complete."

Eventually the book trust was dissolved and replaced by competing firms who for a variety of reasons, including smaller financial resources, were slow to improve the schoolbooks they produced. Nevertheless, the exigencies of competition, the spread of technology, the growing need for a better-educated citizenry, and the persuasive influence of the educational pragmatists did force some significant changes in the schoolbooks used during the first half of the twentieth century. By 1910 John Dewey's advocacy of a child-centered education had begun to take hold, and by 1918 every state had passed a compulsory education law. Also in the same year the National Education Association Commission on the Reorganization of Secondary Education issued its influential report, which reflected the culmination of the trend toward citizenship education. Textbook publishers, while still ruled by regional prejudices, reacted to all these influences by creating textbooks which would hopefully turn the children of immigrant parents into literate citizens, imbuing them with the middle-class American dream and a fervid, if not imaginative, sense of patriotism.

In keeping with the demand for citizenship training, schools began to introduce separate courses in history and civics, and strictly observed national holidays. The child-centered philosophy found expression in the elementary-school social studies texts which began with the child's home and school and eventually broadened to the neighborhood, city, town, county, state, nation, and finally the world. As previously noted, the spiral approach is still the antiquated pattern that shapes most grade-school social studies texts.

In the teaching of reading the McGuffey-type series was replaced by carefully graduated texts using strict vocabulary control. There was less emphasis on fables and myths and more stories about the mishaps and adventures of boys and girls who were the same age as the children reading the schoolbooks. Eventually Dick and Jane and Alice and Jerry and a host of other white, middle-class, idealized families began romping before an ever-growing population of urban children from immigrant homes. The maxims of honesty, fair play, and hard work which Webster and McGuffey had put in their books were still presented, though they were implied rather than explicitly stated.

There were other changes, too, according to Grant Bennion, who three decades ago taught high-school geography and history in Salt Lake City. At the age of twenty Bennion became a salesman for Ginn in Boston. Now president of Ginn, one of the nation's most successful schoolbook publishers, Bennion can look back on more than thirty years of textbook history. "In the 1920's," he recalled, "the textbook stood alone. In the 1930's we began adding extensive teacher manuals and workbooks. In the 1940's we offered black-and-white and color filmstrips and movies. Then came programed instruction in the 1950's. At the same time the textbook itself vastly changed. There were far more provisions for individual differences, graded exercises, and keyed bibliographies."

Actually most of these changes, though not without importance, contained only a few significant improvements. (It has been said that until the present decade the shortest time it has taken to get a new idea accepted in the schools was eighteen years. The subject introduced was driver education.) The forces that worked against change were many—

teachers wedded to old methods and outdated knowledge; the public's unwillingness to seek change or accept the teaching of any topic which might be considered controversial; and the textbook industry's unwillingness or inability to invest in innovation and its deep involvement in a profit structure tied to the big-selling schoolbooks.

Then came a new set of forces which were to provide the seeds for an educational revolution. First nurtured by the scientific and technological shock brought about by World War II, they came to fruition in the competition of the Cold War and through the intense concern of a few brilliant educators like Dr. Jerome Bruner, the director of Harvard's Center for Cognitive Studies, and Dr. Jerrold Zacharias, the M.I.T. physicist. It had finally become apparent that the schools of the 1950's were failing to prepare the nation's children for the complexities of the new age. The knowledge explosion which was to double in the decade separating 1950 and 1960 could overwhelm the world's most advanced technological society if future generations were incapable of coping with the new skills demanded of them. Moreover, because there was so much to learn, children could no longer be expected to absorb all the additional information, facts, and theories which poured in a torrent from the laboratories, the universities, and industry. The knowledge explosion combined with its instant dissemination, writes Charles E. Silberman in *Fortune*, "has utterly destroyed the old conception of school as the place where a person accumulates most of the knowledge he will need over his lifetime. Much of the knowledge today's students will need hasn't been discovered yet, and much of what is now being taught is (or may soon become) obsolete or irrelevant. What students need most, therefore, is not more information but greater depth of understanding, and greater ability to apply that understanding to new situations as they arise."

In November, 1956, a solution was suggested when the

federal government made its first grant for textbook development. Since then the government has given over $41 million to scholars and teachers who have created new teaching techniques and textbooks and teacher's guides in high-school physics, biology, chemistry, foreign languages, and elementary- and high-school mathematics. Most of this money was funneled through the National Science Foundation, an independent agency of the federal government. Once the books with their new approaches to learning were written and tested in the schools, they were then turned over to commercial textbook publishers who sold the books and paid a royalty to the government. At the same time additional millions in government funds were poured into teacher retraining programs.

An instructive illustration of the educational revolution that is taking place—and some of the problems educators still face—can be seen in the achievements and the difficulties that beset the Biological Sciences Curriculum Study (BSCS), a non-profit, independent group of scientists and teachers who have dramatically changed the teaching of high-school biology. Established by the American Institute of Biological Sciences in January, 1959, the BSCS spent four years and nearly eight million dollars in federal funds developing, writing, and testing three new biology textbooks, laboratory guides, and teacher's manuals.

Prior to the publication of the BSCS biology books in 1963, the typical high-school student spent endless hours memorizing the names of animals and plants and analyzing the tissue and cell structures of hearts, brains, stomachs, and livers. Little attention was given to laboratory experiments on how scientists think. Under the BSCS program, today's tenth-grade students spend twice as much time in the laboratory, where they are taught to cross fruit flies to learn about sex-linked inheritance and where they inject male chickens with testosterone to discover the effects of reproductive hormones.

Furthermore, in the texts themselves the youngsters study human reproduction, birth control, race and intelligence and evolution, topics which until 1963 were considered too controversial by most publishers and many teachers.

To ensure that it would produce the finest biology texts possible, BSCS conducted one of the most massive and thorough writing and testing programs in the history of textbook publishing. The study group hired one hundred high-school biology teachers and university research biologists who spent two summers at the University of Colorado in Boulder writing and rewriting the original manuscripts. To test the material, BSCS then put the unfinished books into the hands of 150,000 students in one thousand schools in forty-seven states. The thousands of teachers who taught the new biology compiled extensive reports on how well the youngsters understood the material. All of these comments, as well as reviews written by twenty-five national biological and educational societies, were sent back to the BSCS in Boulder where three teams of seven writers spent as many months preparing the material for commercial publication. The three different textbooks that emerged shared a common content of about 70 percent. Each book also offered its own special approach to biology. *Biological Science: An Inquiry into Life*, which Harcourt, Brace eventually published, stresses cellular analysis; Rand McNally's *High School Biology, BSCS Green Version* covers ecology, the interrelationship between organisms and their environment, and Houghton Mifflin's *Biological Science: Molecules to Man* emphasizes molecular analysis.

Even though the BSCS calls for a more sophisticated teaching approach, the textbooks have proved a success in the schools. Nationwide teacher acceptance was largely won through intensive workshop and training programs sponsored by the BSCS itself, federal and state governments, universities, local school systems, and the publishers. As a result, three out of four schools which have adopted new biology texts since 1963 have chosen BSCS materials. This means that by 1965 some 700,000 out of 2,000,000 tenth graders were learning biology the new way, and by the end of 1967 that figure could leap to 1,600,000 students.

"I do not believe," said Arnold B. Grobman, former BSCS director, "private textbook publishers, by themselves, could afford to invest eight million dollars in such an exhaustive developmental program. I doubt, also, even were the money available, whether such high-caliber biologists and teachers would respond to an appeal from a commercial publisher even though they were pleased to do so for a non-profit scientific organization. The publishers, while many have admirable educational goals, are nevertheless concerned about a marketplace economy and they do react to a minority of dissidence and do adjust their books accordingly. For example, eighty percent of the biology books in American high schools, before the advent of the BSCS, did not even include evolution in their indices despite the fact that the concept has been with us in a fairly rigorous form for over a hundred years. Human reproduction was often omitted, and I recall no adequate discussion of the biological basis for human racial differences. Finally, publishers could have mounted such studies at any time, yet none have done so—at least in science."

While the BSCS represents a great forward leap in textbook publishing, the new biology program also reflects some of the hurdles even the most eminent educators must overcome before they can get their books accepted by the schools. The trouble began with the way the BSCS dealt with sex and culminated in an extraordinary "Monkey War" fought on the battlefields of Texas.

CHAPTER *10*

Texas: King Censor

THE SCIENTISTS AND EDUCATORS at Boulder, Colorado, realized from the start their most difficult fight would be winning acceptance of material that had been considered controversial in the past. One of the BSCS's first battles raged around an illustrated account of human reproduction, a startling advance over conventional high-school texts which, until 1963, rarely went beyond the sex life of sunflowers and earthworms.

As part of its nationwide testing program in 1961, BSCS sent 2,300 orange-covered copies of what was to become *Molecules to Man* to ten schools in Dade County, Florida. Shortly before Christmas county school officials became alarmed when they discovered that the experimental textbooks contained two diagrams of the human male and female reproductive systems. "When we got the book," said Dade County School Superintendent Joe Hall, "we studied it in terms of the Dade School Board policy, which says any sex education must be given to older boys and girls in separate groups." (The school system's biology courses were coeducational.)

"There is a question," he added, "whether this material is sex education or embryology."

To solve their dilemma school authorities asked the BSCS to remove the offending illustrations. When this request was denied, they then threatened to slice out the pages with a razor. But the BSCS explained that the books were the property of the study group, not the school, and the pages could not be deleted. Undaunted, school officials proceeded to hand the 2,300 copies to a group of teachers who spent their Christmas vacation blacking out the illustrations with crayons. When school reopened, the teachers then distributed the censored texts to the children.

"You can imagine the chagrin among the officials," said Arnold Grobman, "when the students quickly discovered that they could view the pictures very easily by holding the books up to the light. I suspect this made the pictures even more interesting, and perhaps there is an educational lesson here. Some parents objected to the pictures having been blacked out, and the school system responded by sending us a rush order for twenty-five additional, unadulterated copies. I suppose that one could then say to the students that the only place to see the 'dirty pictures' was in the school library. Finally some saneness prevailed and the books are now widely used in Miami with the 'offensive' illustrations found on pages two seventy-nine and two eighty of the commercial edition."

The Dade County attack proved only a preliminary skirmish. The major battles occurred after the books were published and focused on the text's defense and full-length treatment of Charles Darwin's theory of evolution.

The fight over whether evolution should be taught in American schools first made national headlines in 1925 when Tennessee charged John Thomas Scopes, a diffident science teacher and football coach, with breaking a new state law that forbade any teacher in a publicly supported school from teaching "any theory that denies the story of the Divine creation of man as taught in the Bible and to teach instead that man has descended from a lower order of animals."

Held in the tiny town of Dayton, Tennessee, the great "Monkey Trial" attracted thousands of spectators, a Ringling Brothers advance man who appeared with a troupe of apes, a Hong Kong journalist and two of the most famous orators of the time: Clarence Darrow, who appeared for the defense, and William Jennings Bryan, a three-time losing presidential candidate who took over the prosecution. For twelve sweltering days the two men clashed, and in the end the jury found Scopes guilty and the judge fined him $100. A year later the Tennessee Supreme Court reversed Scopes's conviction on a legal technicality but left untested the state's anti-evolution law. Ironically, the young teacher, who had voluntarily served as a test case, had been absent from school on the day cited in the indictment and thus never taught the lesson on evolution.

In May, 1967, forty-two years after the Scopes trial, the Tennessee Legislature finally repealed the state's anti-evolution law. However, similar statutes are still in force in Arkansas and Mississippi. Although Louisiana does not have an anti-evolution statute, the state's attitude was summed up by Hubert S. Bankston, assistant state supervisor of elementary science, in June, 1965. "Since there is a tremendous feeling regarding the teaching of evolution in the public schools," he declared, "and since there is so much else of great importance to teach besides the theory of evolution, it is the part of wisdom to avoid the topic just as much as possible." The topic is also avoided in Alabama where the state commissioner of education insisted the BSCS books would not be used in the state's schools as long as he was in office. Despite the commissioner's stand, the city of Mobile purchased three thousand copies. The books were adopted in New Mexico, but the State Board of Education insisted that the inside of the front covers had to be stamped with a legend addressed "To the Users of This Book." Each student and teacher was then told that it is the official position of the Board that "the theory of evolution should be presented as theory only and not as fact."

Along with these anti-evolution tremors, the BSCS experienced shock waves in Kentucky, California, and Arizona. Finally, in the summer of 1964, the "Down with Darwin" earthquake struck in full force. More than four decades after the Scopes trial and 105 years since Darwin first announced his theories of evolution, the Lone Star State held its own belated "Monkey Trial."

Before describing these events and their outcome, let us pause briefly to consider why Texas can force publishers to change the content of their schoolbooks and how textbook censorship works in Texas.

In all the eastern states and throughout most of the Midwest and Far West textbook publishers sell their wares in what is known as open territory. This means that in each of these states each school or district selects the books its children will use. There is no central state authority which must first approve the textbooks that the schools will eventually buy. In contrast almost all of the southern and most of the southwestern states appoint state screening committees which must first select or approve the textbooks before the individual schools can buy them.

Most publishers prefer to offer their texts in an open territory because no state official or single selection committee can prevent them from selling their books to other schools in the state. In contrast, in many of the state adoption systems (twenty-five states in the elementary field and nineteen on the high-school level) the publisher has little chance of selling his books to the individual schools if the state screening committee has failed to give the texts its stamp of approval.

Moreover, under a state adoption system, a small group of officials or a state textbook selection committee can wield a considerable amount of economic power over the publisher. Thus, if one state provides a large enough market for a textbook, it can ask and sometimes get a publisher to change the content of the schoolbook it decides to buy. And because publishers find it less costly to issue a single, nationwide edition, they will frequently incorporate these changes in future printings sold throughout the country. In short, it is possible for one state to determine the content of textbooks used from Maine to Oregon. And on occasion the state of Texas does just that.

A key to this state's influence over publishers can be found at the Texas School Book Depository, a huge seven-story orange brick warehouse in Dallas, which I visited in the spring of 1965. For most people this warehouse crammed with children's schoolbooks serves only as a reminder of the tragic events that took place such a short time ago. Every day visitors would come as they once came to Ford's Theater. They stared at the block-long rows of windows, more faceless than ever since the Depository's directors decided to spruce up the building by covering the panes with Venetian blinds.

But even with so little to see, the tourists continued to arrive, like the bronzed young man in brown slacks and sports shirt who approached the building, only to be stopped by the black and red sign at the entrance: "No Admittance Except for Official Business." Stepping backward, he raised his camera and aimed it at a sixth-floor corner window. There was a slight clicking sound. He had just taken a picture of the exact spot where an unknown order filler sat on a carton of "Think and Do" workbooks and assassinated a President of the United States.

"I have been offered thousands of dollars to retell the story of that day," said Jack Cason, the president of the privately owned Depository. "But I have turned down the offers. We have had enough publicity."

What interests Jack Cason is the serpentine river of textbooks that flows annually from six warehouses into the state's schools. Though he has been in the business for over thirty years, he is still awed by the logistics of loading seventeen six-wheeler vans just for Houston. And this shipment, Cason added, represented only a fraction of the more than $16 million worth of schoolbooks Texas bought the previous year.

However, the huge size of the Texas market does not fully explain the state's influence over publishers. In contrast to states like New York, Pennsylvania, and Illinois, where each school district selects its own books, Texas each year sets up a screening committee of fifteen educators who select textbooks for about 15 percent of the subjects taught in the state's public schools. The Texas committee can recommend up to five schoolbooks in each subject, and this list then goes to the State Board of Education for final approval. Since all the textbooks the Board approves are paid for with state funds, the local schools invariably choose from among those books both the committee and Board of Education have sanctioned. Thus the only way a publisher can hope to partake of the largest state-controlled market in the country is to win the approval of the state's officials. And if approval hinges on a firm's willingness to revise the text, the publisher usually bows to the textbook authorities' demands.

And state authorities do insist upon changes. Under Texas law every publisher who submits a textbook for adoption must sign a contract in which he agrees "to make revisions in content as the State Board of Education may direct, authorize, and demand." If the publisher fails to make the changes, his textbook will automatically be rejected and he will be penalized $2,500. According to Texas authorities, few publishers have failed to make the alterations demanded by the state's officials.

In addition, Texas is the only state that insists upon approving the political affiliations of the books' authors. Before a textbook is accepted in Texas, the authors must first sign an oath swearing they have never belonged to the Communist party or any organization on the U. S. Attorney General's subversive list during the past five years. There is even a provision for dead or missing authors. It is then up to the publisher to swear that the textbook represents the work of a loyal citizen.

According to J. B. Golden, the affable director of the textbook division of the Texas Education Agency, only one author has ever refused to sign the oath since it became a state law in 1953. The publisher then withdrew the book, a seventh-grade science text. "The loyalty oath," Golden said in Austin, "is just a chance for every good American to go up and pledge allegiance. It is also a trap for Communists. If we lay enough of these traps around the country, we are going to get them sooner or later."

Donald Barr, a New York City principal and author of two books adopted by Texas, commented, "Every author or publisher of every schoolbook in the Texas School Book Depository signed an oath swearing he is a loyal American. But Oswald had signed nothing. He had simply never written a textbook."

Actually the textbook loyalty oath has failed to unmask anyone. "I think a Communist will sign anything," explained Golden, a former school superintendent. "Whenever a citizen accuses an author at a textbook hearing," he added, "we run right out to the state Public Safety Department to see if they have a file on him." So far no one has turned up on a list.

Where state authorities have managed to root out alleged "subversives" is in the textbooks themselves. According to

Dr. Lee Wilborn, assistant state commissioner for instruction, one textbook committee succeeded in having removed from seventh- and eighth-grade vocal music books "all references to and works by" noted folk singer Pete Seeger and Negro poet Langston Hughes.

While most of the revisions consist of changing factual errors (one publisher printed the picture of a fire extinguisher upside down), other alterations can affect the tone and character of a book. In 1961, Texas decided to readopt *The American Continents*, a fifth-grade geography text. A year later a new edition appeared in the schools.

In the original version the authors had written: "The United States sometimes finds it difficult to agree with its neighbors in all things. Nor do other countries always agree with us."

In the revised version these two sentences were changed to read: "The people of some nations have forms of government different from ours. Often they do not enjoy the same freedom and opportunity as our people."

Again in the original version the authors said: "But we must keep on trying to find agreement for the good of all. This is one important reason why the United States takes part in the United Nations. There, almost a hundred nations meet to talk about their problems. Only when all nations learn to work together in solving their problems can we be sure of lasting peace in the world."

In the revised edition the passage was altered to read: "Membership in the United Nations brings the United States into contact with almost one hundred foreign nations. The representatives of all these nations meet together at the United Nations headquarters in New York City to discuss international problems. The United States Government, through its representatives, has taken a leading part in the activities in the United Nations."

It is the opinion of Craig T. Senft, president of Silver Burdett, the book's publisher, that these and other changes "tighten up the text in a desirable manner" and "do not significantly change the original intent." According to the company's president, the revisions were incorporated into the 1962 nationwide edition. Furthermore, a new edition published in 1964 containing the altered version is now being sold to schools throughout the country.

Not surprisingly many of the revisions demanded by Texas reflect the political hue of the state. "Texas is fairly conservative," explained King Burney, the southwestern manager for Harcourt, Brace & World. "With a lot of people in Texas the United Nations is a bad name. Therefore, in our history books we treat the U.N. as a fact which it is. We do a minimum of editorializing. That kind of thing Texas people look on pretty critically."

Before publishing its social science and history books, Harcourt, Brace asks some of its salesmen to read the texts while they are still in galley form. "I try to make most of my suggestions for changes before the books are published," King Burney said. "Right now I am reading a civics book which I am checking for controversial material." Then he added ruefully, "Everything is controversial these days."

Declared Bill Jovanovich, Harcourt's president, "The galleys are examined for two things. We are interested in the didactic questions, whether a chapter is too long or too difficult, or whether there is too much emphasis on the pre-Civil War period. Keeping in mind we must be bland in language to please everyone, we look for key words or phrases that might be offensive. Anything that has to do with miscegenation is dangerous as hell. Or anything to do with kinky hair. 'Kinky' is a good Anglo-Saxon word, but in a textbook it becomes highly inflammatory. Nor could you call any American legislation in this country socialist. I can't imagine, for instance, that you could say the Jews who came to the East Side brought some of Bismarck's socialistic ideas which Al Smith took up and got through the New York legislature."

"We must be alert to taboos," added Donald Stewart, editor of Harcourt's *Rise of the American Nation.* "This does not mean a bland mishmash. But it does mean we have to say on the one hand this and on the other hand that. Was the Mexican War a blatant conquest of another people? In New York City we might study it that way, but not in the Southwest or in Texas. In American history the era of controversy begins with McKinley and includes the New Deal, TVA, and Joseph McCarthy."

Sometimes a text's point of view will make an about-face after it has been sharply criticized by a major religious force in Texas. Such was the case with Harcourt's *Men and Nations,* a tenth-grade world history. The book had been in the state's history classrooms for one year without anyone raising an objection. Then in 1963 several members of the Church of Christ, a Protestant sect, charged the text preached "Roman Catholic doctrine." The textbook had portrayed Peter as the founder of the church at Rome. "This is popular legend and a Catholic tradition," said the book's critics, "but is not historical fact."

The Texas Board of Education, which ultimately received the complaint, appointed a committee to re-examine the text. "I worked with Dr. Lee Wilborn of the Texas Education Agency," King Burney recalled, "and Dr. Wilborn said the committee had suggested that if we made certain minor changes we would have a better book and a book less subject to criticism."

In its revision of the offending chapter the publisher replaced an illustration of Peter shown holding "the Gospels and the keys to heaven" with a Rembrandt painting of Paul meditating in a Jerusalem jail. Harcourt also deleted all reference to "St. Peter, leader of the apostles and first bishop of the church at Rome." These and other changes were published in a separately printed chapter which was eventually passed on to the Texas teachers and students using the text. In 1964, Harcourt, Brace & World incorporated the changes in a new edition, and it is this edition which schools throughout the country are now using.

"I cannot say that the original text was untrue," declared King Burney. "We were changing a debatable point which cannot be proven or unproven. Changing the wording meant that we would not anger a large group of people. In a religious argument you can't win."

Commented William Jovanovich, "It is startling to us liberals that not only Jews, Catholics, and Negroes may have a point. We're not given to being sensitive to Protestant objections. In this case I think the critics were historically correct and I made the final decision to insert the changes.

"In a secular society," he added, "it is difficult for a historian to find the historical facts when he seeks truth in myth and religion. This was an instance where there was a meeting of the sales and editorial point of view. But I really can't say whether the truth can be served when history deals with religion."

Men and Nations was altered after the Texas Board of Education approved the book. Usually the state textbook selection committee compiles a list of suggested revisions and then hands them to the publisher a crucial three to four weeks before the State Board decides whether it will adopt the textbook. At this point one of the state's curriculum experts attempts to negotiate the change with the publisher. "We have some competent people and they don't just give in," said state textbook director Golden. "If the author's opinion is in question, we prevail."

There have been occasions, though, when the state's curriculum experts and the selection committees have upheld the authors and publishers. For instance, one angry citizen tried but failed to get a textbook committee to remove the spiritual "He's Got the Whole World in His Hands" from a song book because it fostered one-worldism. A more serious criticism was leveled at Macmillan's *Government in Our Republic,* a civil government textbook for high-school students which Texas wanted to adopt in 1964. A textbook committee member took issue with a paragraph that suggested Congressional committees had abused their power. The passage, said the committee members, was "loaded" and "not objective."

In a letter to Macmillan, the Texas Education Agency wrote, "Anyone old enough to remember Senator McCarthy's investigations recalls that abuses have occurred. We see no reason to ask the publisher to change statements in this paragraph." As a result no change was made and the book was adopted. "If you are telling the whole story," said Dr. W. R. Goodson, head of the state's curriculum development department, "you should say a change is not made every time a criticism is raised in Texas. At the same time, the effect is to keep controversial issues from being presented. Our staff, however, tries to avoid that approach."

But the state's curriculum experts do not always succeed in keeping the censors at bay. Indeed, such was the case when the three BSCS books came up for possible selection. Despite the extensive reviews of the three textbooks conducted by many of the nation's top scientists, six passages in *Molecules to Man,* issued by Houghton Mifflin, were altered after all three books had been printed, bound, and sold in other states. The six passages, all of which dealt with evolution, were changed after the books had been submitted for adoption in Texas. Several leading scientists have described the changes at best as a watering down of the text and at worst as giving students a misleading picture of biology's most basic theory.

The man who set off the Texas "Monkey Trial" is a mild-mannered, gray-haired, fifty-three-year-old preacher named Reuel Lemmons. Lemmons, who lives in Austin, edits *Firm Foundation,* a weekly newspaper which is mailed to 40,000 members of the Church of Christ, a huge fundamentalist sect with over 600,000 adherents in Texas alone.

In the spring of 1964, Lemmons had learned that Texas was considering adopting the BSCS books. Girding for battle, the preacher wrote a scathing editorial which *Firm Foundation* published on June 30. Entitled "An Extremely Dangerous Biology Textbook Coming," the editorial described the BSCS texts as "Godless" and "atheistic." However, Lemmons' greatest ire was reserved for Houghton Mifflin's *Molecules to Man.*

"It is pure evolution from cover to cover, completely materialistic and completely atheistic," he thundered. "Unless something is done quickly these are the texts your children will be studying in biology next fall." At the end of the editorial he asked his readers to petition, phone, and write their congressman, the Texas Education Agency, newspapers, the P.T.A. and local school boards, and superintendents. "It is just possible," he concluded, "that enough public opinion can be mustered to get these Godless texts rejected if they cannot be changed."

The response was extraordinary even for Texas whose citizens are encouraged by state authorities to protest against the adoption of any textbook they do not like. During the campaign which lasted through the summer and fall, the fundamentalists made speeches on the radio, collected hundreds of petitions, and bombarded state and local officials with thousands of letters. They even suggested that the "atheistic" theories of Charles Darwin could produce another Lee Harvey Oswald. In a stream of form letters sent to Governor John Connally, the anti-evolutionists declared, "The assassination of our late President and the attempt upon your life were the vicious acts of a Godless individual. It is the purpose of this letter to call your attention to a situation in our state which is designed to promote such Godlessness in our public schools through the atheistic teaching of the 'evolutionary theory.'" At the Texas Education Agency the letters and petitions filled two huge cartons. "It was," said J. B. Golden, "the most voluminous protest in my eleven years with the Agency."

The fundamentalist attack reached fever pitch on October 14, when the state selection committee conducted its annual public textbook hearing. The hearing was held in a Texas Education Agency conference room crammed with folding chairs and TV cameras. By 9 A.M. more than two hundred people had gathered in the room. Facing the audience were the fifteen textbook committee members who had already taken their seats around a long U-shaped table.

The hearing began with the intoning of a prayer asking God's guidance in the committee's deliberations. One of the first witnesses was Reuel Lemmons. A tall, spare man, he stepped before the committee and declared, "If the first amendment forbids the teaching of the Bible's account of creation, then that same amendment should forbid the teaching of an anti-creation theory." Reaching his peroration, the preacher warned, "This theory [of evolution] which these texts would teach our children for many years to come will undermine faith in God and in the spiritual and to that extent undermine America whose motto is—'In God We Trust.'" Lemmons was followed by a farmer, a housewife, a dentist, and two college professors, eventually over a dozen witnesses in all, who sought to have the textbooks banned or changed.

As the publishers' salesmen and editors rose to the defense of the textbooks, they tried to mollify the critics by reaffirming that no atheist had a hand in writing, producing, or selling the BSCS material. "The authors," declared Gordon Hjalmarson, the BSCS editor at Houghton Mifflin, "are for most cases native-born American Christians. They themselves as Mr. Brown [the firm's top Texas salesman] has indicated, he teaches Sunday School in Dallas [sic]. The supervisor of the Blue Version writing team representing the Biological Sciences Curriculum Study, Dr. [Claude] Welch, has been an elder in the United Church of Christ. I am at the present time and have been for the last two years a deacon in the local Congregational Church in my home town."

That night the witnesses watched themselves on the Huntley-Brinkley show.

"I will tell you," said Dr. Irwin Spear, associate professor of botany at the University of Texas in Austin, "I was worried. So was everyone else." Though Dr. Spear had wanted to testify in behalf of the BSCS texts, he had not been given permission. Under the committee's rules, only the critics of the books could bring in outside experts. "The critics said the books were bad science," Dr. Spear added, "yet nobody like myself could get up and refute these statements. I wanted to tell them I am a college biology teacher and I am concerned about my students' science backgrounds, and I wanted to say, too, that I am a parent and I want my kids to be taught evolution."

The next day the selection committee met in secret. During the early deliberations it seemed that the fundamentalists had won a partial victory. Eight different biology books had been submitted to the committee, which could only choose five, and at first the members were prepared to reject at least one and possibly two of the BSCS texts. On the following day the state selection committee announced its decision to the press. It had recommended not one but all three of the new biology books. "It was a very intelligent group," explained a committee member who asked not to be identified. One of the most highly respected teachers in Texas, this member had argued that the state would be failing its students if it turned down the BSCS books. "Maybe," said the teacher, "I persuaded a good bit."

The battle, however, was not over. Dr. J. W. Edgar, the state commissioner of education, could remove three of the five biology books the committee had recommended. Again the fundamentalists protested, but the commissioner upheld the committee's selections. The final decision now rested with the twenty-one elected members of the State Board of Education. Another campaign, another hearing, and finally in November, 1964, the *Sweetwater Texas Reporter* emblazoned its edition with the headline: "Darwin Declared Winner in Texas 'Monkey War.'"

But the Texas "Monkey War" was not without its casualties. In their campaign the fundamentalists had reserved their greatest fury for Houghton Mifflin's *Molecules to Man*, which went further than any of the other BSCS texts in presenting Darwin's theory. As a result, several textbook committee members and their advisers pointed out to the firm's Texas salesmen that in order to get the book approved by the state and adopted by the local schools, the publisher would have to make a number of changes involving evolution. As George M. Fenollosa, vice-president of Houghton Mifflin, put it, "In any selling situation the salesman wants to give customers what they want. If the customer wants strawberries and cream, the salesman tries to give it to him."

But the salesmen were in a bind. No changes could be

made without the approval of the Biological Sciences Curriculum Study. The only recourse was to send the Texas comments to the firm's home office in Boston, which in turn forwarded them to Michigan State University's Claude Welch, the BSCS writing supervisor of *Molecules to Man*.

On October 2, some twelve days before the selection committee held its public hearing, Mr. Fay Brown, the manager of Houghton Mifflin's Dallas office, wrote the state commissioner of education that the changes would be made. In his letter Brown declared: "Even though 'Molecules to Man' represents the most thoroughly tested project in history, the authors and publishers welcome any constructive suggestions which will enhance the scientific-inquiry approach to biology for all students." The changes Fay Brown listed as enhancing scientific-inquiry include the following:

In the original version the authors had written: "Evolution is not a faith, but a scientific theory. The theory has been developed to account for a body of facts."

This was changed to read: "Evolution is not a *belief*, nor an *observational fact*—it is a scientific theory." (The anti-evolutionists had complained that if students were told evolution is a fact they would no longer believe in the Bible and Divine creation.)

Declared Dr. Irwin Spear, "It changes a perfectly accurate statement into, at best, an ambiguous and fuzzy statement that most biologists would consider misleading if not inaccurate. Evolution has been observed as an experimental fact and most of us give lectures on cases where evolution has been observed." Added Dr. George Gaylord Simpson, Alexander Agassiz Professor of Vertebrate Paleontology at Harvard University: "The anti-evolutionist can always define away a statement that evolution *is* a fact. The late William Jennings Bryan's idea of evolution as a fact was that one should be able to sit down in the garden and watch an onion turning into a lily. Such ignorance plus disingenuousness is virtually unassailable."

In another change the publisher and Dr. Welch had substituted the word "modified" for "strengthened" in the sentence, "Like all scientific theory, the theory of evolution has been both strengthened [now read 'modified'] and revised as research disclosed more and more facts."

Professor Simpson described the change as weakening the statement in a "misleading way and undoubtedly is meant to do so." He added, not a single biological discovery before or since Darwin has "weakened" the evidence for evolution. "On the contrary," he declared, "the evidence has been enormously strengthened since Darwin."

In still other changes the BSCS replaced, "Biologists are *convinced* that the human species evolved from nonhuman forms," with the sentence, "Many biologists *assume* that the human species evolved from nonhuman forms." They also deleted the sentence, "To biologists there is no longer any reasonable doubt that evolution occurs." This deleted sentence, Dr. Spear commented, "is perfectly valid" and "represents the viewpoint of *at least* ninety-nine percent of all biologists."

Dr. Claude Welch, who authorized the changes, insists they are "minor" and in no way "reduced the logic of our presentation of evolution." Of the pages upon pages of requests for revisions submitted by teachers and private citizens, he declared he "flatly rejected" 99.9 percent of them. "I approved the ones listed in [Fay] Brown's letter," Dr. Welch went on, "simply because the changes seem to make good sense. I certainly don't see what the fuss is about."

In the opinion of Professor Simpson, one of the nation's top scientists, "the fuss" transcends Darwin's theory. "With only one exception," he declared, "the changes follow a tradition of ignorant, red-neck anti-rationalism and antievolutionism. They deliberately batten on the vulgar misapprehension that a scientific theory is guesswork, hence as likely to be wrong as right." He added that such a view "is particularly dangerous when it is incorporated in a young person's study of science, which should show him, at least, the rudiments of rational thinking in the scientific way."

While this reporter does not cavil with Professor Simpson's comments, it must be added that, even with these alterations, *Molecules to Man,* as well as the other two BSCS texts, covers evolution in considerable depth. It must also be noted that they present such topics as human reproduction, birth control, and race and intelligence, all previously considered taboo. As Dr. Theodosius Dobzhansky, one of the country's most eminent geneticists and evolutionists, commented, "What progress in comparison to the situation which prevailed before the BSCS texts appeared." Finally, it must not be forgotten that despite one of the most vigorous protests ever conducted by an aroused citizenry against textbooks, Texas itself approved all three BSCS books and nearly half the schools chose these texts from among the five the State Board of Education had sanctioned.

Yet with all this one must emphasize that the dubious changes made as the result of the Texas adoption will be incorporated into future printings which will be sold to schools throughout the United States. As previously noted, this is common practice.

In 1961 and 1962, Jack Nelson, a Pulitzer prizewinning journalist from Atlanta, Georgia, and Gene Roberts, Jr., a reporter for the Raleigh, North Carolina, *News and Observer,* made an exhaustive study of textbook censorship which they published in *The Censors and the Schools.* They ended their book by quoting from an editorial that appeared in the Winston-Salem, North Carolina, *Journal.*

"It is one thing," the newspaper declared, "to express

honest criticism of some school text or teaching program and raise public questions about it. It is quite another thing to use group pressure to have certain materials banned because they do not conform to some special group's ideas about Americanism, minority group interests, or whatnot. If we allow pressure groups, rather than our qualified educators, to determine the content of schoolbooks, teaching in our schools will soon degenerate into indoctrination, with facts being embroidered with propaganda and truth tailored to fit some super-zealot's pet prejudice or theory."

Commented the authors in 1963, "The prospect, to say the least, is a forbidding one." Though it seems less forbidding today, the "tradition of ignorant, red-neck anti-rationalism" still infects many communities and schools and the textbooks your children may use.

CHAPTER 11

"Can a Child Ask the Moon?"

HIS GREETING WAS WARM, almost effusive, his informal attire typically professional, a red jacket over a bright red tie rippling down a gray shirt. His silver hair was parted in the middle. Festooned along one wall of his spacious office were group photographs of the nation's most eminent scientists, all friends or acquaintances of the man I had come to see, Dr. Jerrold R. Zacharias, professor of physics at M.I.T.

During most of his academic career, Dr. Zacharias had been absorbed by such esoteric fields of research as the hyperfine structure of atomic hydrogen, deuterium, and chlorine and the nuclear moments of those elements and their isotopes. He was one of the developers of the atomic beam clock, an extraordinarily precise device that loses only one-hundredth of a second a year. More recently, however, he has been consumed by problems of a more serious nature. Not along ago he developed a microbalance consisting of a drinking straw and needles which proved so sensitive it could weigh a fly's wing. With the aid of such simple devices Dr. Zacharias and his colleagues have already wrought an educational revolution. The story of what can only be described as a momentous crusade to reform the curriculum of the nation's grade and high schools begins with its originator and driving force.

"I lived through the Hitler times," Professor Zacharias recalled that day, "though I lost no relatives in the Hitler murders. I have always felt bitter about lying and the exploitation of the big lie. As professional scientists we cannot lie. We can make mistakes a dime a dozen. But we cannot lie. Even the Russians as scientists know this. When the Russians say they have taken a picture of the other side of the moon we know it is a bona-fide photo. What has lying to do with intellectuality? People must know why they believe what they believe. They must be able to confront evidence, respect it. And this requires intellectuality."

However, in our time and in our country, the anti-intellectuals found sustenance in the tensions of the Cold War and a leader in the late Senator McCarthy. In such an atmosphere the search for truth was frequently considered an act of subversion and the intellectual was looked upon as the purveyor of heresy. During this period, Dr. Zacharias began serving as a member of the committee of scientists which advised the President. Distressed by the public witch hunts, he also witnessed the privately expressed fears of government officials who seemed haunted by the specter of Russian scientific achievements. Then in 1956 Professor Zacharias arose to address his colleagues.

"We had been briefed to the point of boredom on how the Russians were getting ahead of us technologically," he recalled. "Finally I spoke up. The problem was not the Russians, but the anti-intellectualism which had pervaded our colleges and schools and which was getting into our children. 'Shouldn't we understand this problem?' I asked."

At first no one responded.

"The only way I know how to do anything," Professor Zacharias said, "is to start with the specific and go to the general." The specific that he knew best of all was physics. He was concerned, too, with the way this discipline was being taught in the schools. As he later wrote, "The tidy notions of classical mechanics still predominate in the way we try to introduce the subject of physics and it usually happens that these notions are dull as presented because it is so difficult to present arresting experiments to liven them up." He felt that the steam-shovel approach to physics hardly made much sense. "Steam shovels provide a good avenue to learning physics," he declared, "but how many people can get their hands on a steam shovel?" Finally, he was deeply concerned with the textbooks then in use which he felt grossly misrepresented the subject he loved.

On March 15, 1956—a year and a half before the Russians launched Sputnik and the space age—Professor Zacharias composed a now historic memorandum. It was addressed to Dr. James R. Killian, Jr., president of M.I.T. At the time it must have seemed unlikely that this memorandum of a little more than three pages was of such major significance that it would inspire a national commitment. The memorandum began simply:

Subject: *Movie Aids for Teaching Physics in High Schools*
In order to present one subject, say physics, it is proposed that we make 90 films of 20-minutes duration, complete with text books, problem books, question cards and answer cards. Each of these points requires some discussion but before taking up the detailed mechanism it is necessary first to look at the subject matter. Success or failure depends to a large extent on having the entire apparatus of the experiment really right. Like a high fidelity phonograph, one must have besides the machine a good piece by a good composer played by an artist. The room must be good, not too noisy, and the people have to want to listen, but that all depends upon the piece.

The president of M.I.T. encouraged Dr. Zacharias to bring his ideas to the attention of the National Science Foundation. "I showed the memo to Alan Waterman, director of N.S.F., at about three P.M.," the M.I.T. professor said. "By five P.M. Harry Kelly, N.S.F. educational director, was trying to persuade me to pick up the suggestion. I said it would cost three hundred thousand dollars to find out whether you can do it and ten times as much to do it."

Not only the times but the innovator were right for the experiment. In the past most college and university scholars were either absorbed by their own fields of study or were so determined to improve their own academic status that they showed little if any interest in the education offered in the nation's grade and high schools. Now a professor of Jerrold Zacharias's stature wanted to become involved. Moreover, since he was esteemed by his colleagues, Dr. Zacharias might be able to persuade some of the country's most brilliant minds to participate in the experiment. In the generally dismal annals of educational innovation, here was an extraordinary opportunity.

"I knew from the very beginning that this would be a big enough job to get the best working on it from the start," Professor Zacharias said. "I wanted Harvard, Cal Tech, Columbia, Cornell, Bell Telephone Labs, the University of Illinois, and M.I.T. However, none of this was to be done by institutional relationships. It would just be us boys, professional scientists who had worked together."

In the fall of 1956 "us boys" formed the Physical Science Study Committee. Headed by Dr. Zacharias, the PSSC included Dr. Killian and professors from Harvard, Columbia, Bryn Mawr, and M.I.T., Dr. Edwin Land of Land Polaroid, Paul Brandwein of Harcourt, Brace, Henry Chauncey, head of Educational Testing Service, which constructs the College Boards, and Dr. Morris Meister, then principal of the

Bronx High School of Science. By November the National Science Foundation made its first grant of $303,000 to the PSSC. (For the National Science Foundation this sum turned out to be a mere pittance. Eventually the moneys spent by the Foundation on curriculum development swelled to over $40 million, and now in honor of Jerrold Zacharias, the N.S.F. counts its grants in multiples of ZACHS, with each ZACH equivalent to a quarter of a million dollars.)

In December, 1956, PSSC held its first crucial meeting to hammer out guidelines for a new science program. For three days fifty distinguished scientists, educators, high-school teachers, and professional men met in Cambridge, Massachusetts. The meetings were often noisy, the arguments heated. However, when the sessions ended, there was general agreement on a number of basic points.

In brief, it was decided to create an entirely new, one-year course in high-school physics as the discipline was approached by the contemporary scientist. The aim was to allow and encourage the student to *be* a physicist, to learn by exploring and experiment, and thereby to *experience* scientific inquiry in contrast to the old method where the student attempted to absorb the subject as simply one more lesson in a book. All this was to be achieved by a number of devices including: (1) a new and different kind of text that substituted a conceptual narrative of physics for the "technological wizard" approach; (2) open-ended laboratory experiments and inexpensive lab equipment to be used to *explore* the phenomena of nature; (3) following Dr. Zacharias's original memorandum to Dr. Killian, a series of films made by leading physicists demonstrating phenomena, experiments, and concepts that would prove too difficult to explore or create in the high-school lab; (4) a new set of teacher's and lab guides; (5) a series of paperback monographs on topics not covered in other materials, and (6) a new series of exams which tested for conceptual understanding instead of rote learning.

If such an ambitious program had been proposed in the past it probably would have taken two generations or more to get the schools to adopt it. However, within four years the first hardbound new physics textbook began appearing in the classrooms. Along with the text went all the devices just mentioned and suggestions on how to build inexpensive equipment like the microbalance described earlier and a ripple tank made out of an ordinary window frame at a cost of $6, which if it had been manufactured would have been priced at $100. The total cost of developing the PSSC program came to a little over $5 million, almost all of it provided through the National Science Foundation. Part of these funds were used to train teachers in the new physics and to test the program in the schools. Finally, the text was turned over to D. C. Heath, a commercial publisher. Now being used by half of the 500,000 students studying high-school physics, the PSSC text has also been translated by the Russians, who distributed 100,000 copies to future physics teachers in Soviet schools of education.

But the new physics program was only the beginning. Since the National Science Foundation made its first grant to the PSSC in November, 1956, millions in federal funds have been distributed by the N.S.F. to other study groups. In May, 1958, the School Mathematics Study Group received its first N.S.F. grant which has now grown to over $10 million. The mathematicians were followed by the biologists, who received over $7.5 million, the chemists who were given $4 million, and a variety of elementary-science study groups who have received more than $7 million. The result has been a revolution in the teaching of high-school science and grade- and high-school math. Considering the results, the costs, even on occasion if there has been some waste, are remarkably low. As Professor Zacharias put it in his original memorandum to Dr. Killian, "The financial side of such an enterprise becomes obvious on considering the amount of film that will have to be thrown away before a first-rate reel is accomplished. Copies of the films are easy. But the efficiency of Flaubert was not high."

Perhaps the most exciting promise of these new programs is that learning, until recently a deadly mixture of drivel and drudgery, can become a fascinating experience for both teachers and students. Consider what has happened to the teaching of foreign languages, a subject in the past that was learned by rote and taught by drill.

Until 1961 almost every youngster who studied French, German, Spanish, or Russian was given a combination grammar book and reader. "He would spend two years translating sentences like 'My aunt's purple umbrella is under the bench in the park,'" recalled Mary Thompson with a quiver of horror. Miss Thompson, who directed the federally funded language revolution and now heads the language department at Harcourt, Brace, added, "The only objectives in teaching foreign languages were reading and translation. It was a deadening process with no relation to the fact that these are living languages. Few children ever learned how to listen and speak."

Today a child in the seventh grade who takes French under the new program learns to speak before he learns to read and write. Instead of beginning with a grammar book, he starts by listening to a recording of a native speaker who carries on a simple dialogue. The teacher translates the sentences into English and repeats them in French. Then the class speaks the dialogue, but only in the foreign language. This process is repeated at home where the child listens to a record made by a native speaker and again practices the dialogues in French. For the first four months the student is given no textbook, a fact which has horrified many parents who have to be reassured by the teachers that the best way to study a spoken language is to speak it. Finally, around December, the teacher presents the alphabet and begins dictating simple sentences in French. Within two years a youngster is reading excerpts from modern French novels, poetry, and newspapers, and carrying on ordinary conversations in French.

"A youngster who has taken four years under this program," said Miss Thompson, "can go to a French film and understand it. He can listen to a lecture in French in college. If he goes to France, he will understand what is said over the telephone and he should be able to participate in a conversation without sounding ridiculous or grotesque. And if he wishes he should be able to read any book, magazine, or newspaper."

The dramatic changes that are taking place in the teaching of foreign languages, science, and math are only beginning to touch the two vital remaining disciplines, humanities and social studies. But here, too, a whole new world of learning is about to burst upon the schools. As in the sciences, millions of dollars in federal, foundation, and university grants are being poured into over 140 research and development programs in literature, American history, economics, and civics.

At Harvard, Dr. Donald Oliver, a professor of education and a social scientist, is experimenting with a senior-high-school social studies program which is unlike any history or civics course taught in any school anywhere. This course, which is being tried out on Newton, Massachusetts, students who do not plan to go to college, presents the great controversial issues of the past and present. Readings include an excerpt from Kenneth Roberts' novel, *Oliver Wiswell,* describing the persecution of a liberal Tory family by the rebelling Americans, the trial of Galileo Galilei, and an account of how a Boston mob killed a United States marshal who was returning a Negro slave to his owner in the South under the Fugitive Slave Law.

The youngsters are then bombarded with a series of highly charged questions that involve them in conflicts of conscience and values. In the case of the Boston mob and the Fugitive Slave Law they are asked: Should the federal government have the right to make and enforce a law that sends a man back into slavery? If the youngsters answer "No," then they are asked if they would participate in the mob action. If they answer "Yes," then the teacher poses the question: "Should the people who attempt to free the slave be held criminally responsible for the death of the marshal?" The students then must decide whether violence is a legitimate means of protest.

"In the conventional history textbooks," Oliver said, "problems are presented in an orderly, legal framework. Sort of the great melting-pot theory. In this Garden of Eden little or no mention is made of early corporate practices to avoid competition, the disposition of the American Indians, which was close to genocide, the exploitation of immigrants. What we try to show is that society is made up of conflicting interest groups. Society then sets up legal and political institutions which attempt to mediate the differences among these groups. Sometimes, as in the case of the Boston mob and the Fugitive Slave Law, the conflict in values is so extreme that the institutions break down. It is at this point we try to get the youngsters to resolve these conflicts by creating better institutions. Our aim is not to have these kids see society as a jungle. But we don't want them to think it is a Garden of Eden either."

Many scholars echo Dr. Oliver's basic charge that few students are ever taught to think like social scientists. One reason

given by the scholars is that the traditional textbooks attempt
to cover too much history and thus do not have the space to
present more than a brief summary of events which are
wrapped in predigested conclusions. Typically, a high-school
student will spend nine months learning five thousand years
of world history, all of which will be summed up in an 800-
page textbook. Commented Arthur S. Trace, author of *What
Ivan Knows That Johnny Doesn't*, "An American student
who had to stay home with a bad cold could miss out on
Greek civilization, and if he happened to contract pneumonia, he could miss out on the entire ancient world."

The same holds true in the study of American history. "In
the fifth, eighth, and eleventh grades," declares Peter Wolff,
"youngsters study Leif Ericson to Lyndon Johnson. And all
they get is one damned event after another."

Wolff is the forty-two-year-old editorial director of a new
elementary- and high-school social studies program which is
being created by Educational Services, Inc., a non-profit
organization of university scholars and elementary- and
high-school teachers. One of ESI's most exciting projects is
a course on Colonial history for twelve-year-olds that is
based almost entirely on original sources and documents.
The aim is twofold: to teach eighth graders American history
and at the same time to train them to think like historians.

For example, an experimental section on the Battle of
Lexington poses a startlingly simple question which no
elementary- or high-school textbook ever asks: "What happened on April 19, 1775, at Lexington, Massachusetts?"
However, the student quickly learns the answer is not simple.

The lesson begins with the presentation of different paintings portraying the same battle. One picture shows the
Minutemen running from the British guns, another depicts
the militia standing firm while the English soldiers disappear
in a haze of smoke. The student is not told that one painting

was drawn by a British artist and the other is the work of an American. But he is asked to describe the different portrayals.

The youngsters are then given six written versions of the Battle of Lexington. They include three accounts composed by English soldiers, two of whom fought at Lexington, and three others written by Americans who either served with the militia or defended the Minutemen in letters and sermons. The eighth graders are then asked to show where the British and Americans agreed, disagreed, and finally to construct their own version of what happened at the Battle of Lexington. "Without ever being told what is happening to him," said Peter Wolff, "the child learns to think like an historian."

Educational Services, Inc., for whom Wolff works, has headquarters in suburban Boston and is the oldest and largest of the half-dozen independent curriculum-reform groups scattered around the nation.

Founded in 1958, ESI grew out of the Physical Science Study Committee and now not only handles the PSSC but has underway programs that could completely change the teaching of elementary-school science and social studies from kindergarten through the twelfth grade. It has also prepared mathematics materials to be used in ten African nations from Ethiopia and Ghana to Uganda and Zambia.

In keeping with the educational revolution begun by Dr. Zacharias, an increasing number of grade and high schools are seeking and welcoming new ways of teaching almost every subject or are willing to introduce new topics in grades where they have rarely if ever been taught before. As a result, the once staid publishing industry is beginning to issue a variety of different kinds of textbooks and educational materials that are as exciting as anything the curriculum reform groups have created. Though much of this material has been subsidized by the federal government and private foundations, the publishing houses are risking their own money for some of the research and in some cases paying all the costs. Indeed, for the first time in the history of textbook publishing almost every major house can boast of at least one innovation in a field that had barely changed for nearly half a century.

Heath de Rochemont, a division of the Boston publisher D. C. Heath, is teaching French and Spanish to fourth, fifth, and sixth graders with a series of records, workbooks, and eight mm. self-winding films which are shown on a TV-like projector that a five-year-old can operate. Among other things, this program overcomes what had once been the almost insurmountable problem in teaching elementary-school children foreign languages, the grade-school teacher who only spoke English.

In Evanston, Illinois, Harper & Row is producing a series based entirely on linguistics which may change the teaching of reading, and in New York, Harcourt, Brace & World may do the same for the teaching of grammar. Entitled *The Roberts English Series: A Linguistics Program,* for grades three through six, the Harcourt textbooks represent the first major revamping of English grammar since Bishop Robert Lowth wrote the basic text in 1762. The new system, called "transformational grammar," abolishes the Latin-based syntactical rules and substitutes a set of simpler rules and principles which in a logical fashion help a child grasp the subtleties of his own language.

In Boston, Allyn and Bacon has exploded the "one damned event after another" encyclopedic approach to world history by publishing *A Global History of Man* for high-school students. This rather remarkable and unorthodox textbook was created under the direction of L. S. Stavrianos, professor of history at Northwestern University. Development costs, which came to over $144,000, were provided by the Carnegie Corporation of New York. Instead of dwelling almost exclusively on the history of the West, as most world histories do, this schoolbook also explores in depth such areas as China, sub-Sahara Africa, and India. In contrast to the traditional chronological approach, the authors employed a flashback technique which begins with a description of present historical conditions and institutions and then seeks to explain them by describing the historical events and forces that produced them. Finally, each student is given a 908-page supplement of readings ranging from Confucius and Pericles to Khrushchev and Kwame Nkrumah. These essays are intertwined with the text.

According to Professor Stavrianos, A Global History of Man and its supplementary material were rejected by a "large percentage of the publishing firms" before they were accepted by Allyn and Bacon. "The reason usually given," he added, "was that they would prove 'too difficult' for high-school students. Contrary to this judgment, both the text and the reader were widely adopted from the very first year of publication [1962], and the adoptions have increased steadily each year, contrary to the usual textbook pattern."

An even more revolutionary approach to learning is the program which attempts to teach children without a textbook, an unusual venture since it presupposes that the teacher will discard the traditional teaching crutch and rely on an alien device or in some cases on her own skills and imagination. It is unlikely that such approaches to learning will be widely employed in the near future since most teachers are still dependent upon the schoolbooks used by their own students. Nevertheless some promising devices are already on the educational market and more will be forthcoming shortly.

For instance, Science Research Associates in Chicago is

attempting to teach economics, the so-called "dismal science," to first, second, and third graders. Using fairy tales, short stories, and poetry as its source material, *Our Working World*, a schoolbook combined with records, manages to explain such difficult concepts as the division of labor and conditions like unemployment.

Even more promising and perhaps the most important new development to date is Dr. Omar Khayyam Moore's talking typewriter, which he has used to teach children as young as two years of age to read, spell, punctuate, and even touch-type by the time they have reached their third birthday. A child begins to learn by poking at any letter on the keyboard of a specially built electric typewriter. No sooner has he pressed, say, the letter "P" then a tape-recorded voice calls out, "P." After a little more than a week of daily half-hour sessions with the machine the youngster has taught himself the alphabet and the keyboard symbols. Now an attendant adjusts a knob and the youngster finds he can no longer strike the keys at random and get a response. Instead he must wait while the machine announces a letter which also appears on a card above the typewriter. Since all the keys are locked except the one the machine is asking for, the child quickly learns how to match the keys with their sounds and images. Next comes the crucial step when the machine announces a word—D-A-Y—and within a short time the youngster is not only reading but typing out a torrent of words: day, pay, may, way.

Using Dr. Moore's machine, four-year-old children of average intelligence have learned to read, write, and type sentences in three months. In one school, the *Saturday Evening Post* reported, first graders who learned to write on the talking typewriter publish their own newspaper. Their imaginations freed because they have already achieved considerable skill in reading and writing, they can give free rein to their creative impulses. Such was the case with this first grader who produced this delightful account of an evening at Ford's hockey arena:

> Abraham Lincoln got shot. He was watching the hockey game at the fair. Someone had a gun. He shot Abraham Lincoln in the head. They stopped playing hockey and called the ambulance. It came rushing no matter if cars were in front of it or not. They shouted to the boss of the hockey game to call the police. They found the man with the gun.

The six-year-old editors of the newspaper accepted and published the story, but apparently concerned that some of their readers might be confused, they added this editor's note:

> (All of Spencer's story is not true.)

Dr. Moore believes the talking typewriter's success is largely due to the fact the young become highly motivated when they are allowed to learn by making their own "discoveries." * Also the machine has the non-human virtue of never losing its temper and therefore no child who learns to read this way will ever be told that he is dumb, which he is

---

* It should not be too surprising that the most startling innovations in the educational revolution are taking place in the teaching of reading. Besides the talking typewriter and linguistics, children are being taught how to read through ITA, color reading, and in some ways the simplest and most promising device, the blackboard and a piece of chalk, or in its modern form the overhead projector. Here a group of youngsters learn to read by constructing their own stories. As each child adds a sentence the teacher writes it down on a transparency and the projector then flashes the story onto a screen or wall. Children then read the sentences back to the class. The youngsters become highly motivated to learn because the story they are reading is something they created. In the hands of a highly skilled teacher this technique can prove effective in all kinds of classrooms, from those located in the slums to schools in the book-reading culturally exposed suburbs.

told repeatedly, though inferentially, if he is grouped in the bottom third of a reading class using a graded reader. (Those educators who insist upon separating children like cream and milk can never seem to understand why the milk is no longer capable of turning back into cream.)

The discovery method is now employed to teach children math, science, and history. Its most widespread use is probably in science and mathematics, and its most dramatic application can be found in the Cuisenaire Rods, consisting of seventy-two wooden sticks ranging in length from one to ten centimeters. The smallest rod is white, the two-centimeter rod is red, the three-centimeter rod is green, and so on. The children begin by making different play patterns. Soon they discover that rods of the same color are interchangeable and thus have taken their first small step in learning a fundamental mathematical structure, the equivalence relation. As they continue to play with the sticks, they find that by putting two rods end to end they have begun the addition process. Eventually, through the use of different combinations, the youngsters discover with the aid of a teacher all the different mathematical operations, including multiplication, factoring, and division, fractions, and proportion. Along the way they are taught to substitute written numbers and other mathematical symbols. The results at times have been extraordinary. One eight-year-old, asked to multiply 18 × 35, gave eight different ways of solving the problem. Another eight-year-old was asked to make up a problem about a real-life situation and produced the following:

Once I went shopping. I saw 48 marbles and bought two-thirds of them. The other day I found 60 marbles in the street but lost half of them. Playing marbles I won 48 and lost 1/8 of them.

The next day I won 9 and lost 1/3 of them. How many marbles did I have?

(Answer: $2/3 \times 48 + 60 - 1/2 \times 60 + 48 - 1/8 \times 48 + 9 - 1/3 \times 9 = 110$)

Two great virtues of the discovery method are the variety of paths students may take in solving a problem and the improved quality of questions students themselves ask as they go about seeking a solution. One of the simplest and most ingenious projects of this kind is the SRA Inquiry Development Program, which permits elementary-school students to learn how to form a workable hypothesis based on the observation of certain phenomena.

For example, a fifth grade is shown a film of a scientist performing a simple experiment in a laboratory. Using a pair of tongs, the scientist drops a brass ball through a ring. He then holds the ball over a Bunsen burner and, once it has been heated, places the ball on the opening of the ring. That's all ten-year-old Jeffrey saw when his teacher, Ruth Lang, flashed the film on the screen in their classroom in Elk Grove, Illinois. Immediately Jeffrey raised his hand. A tall, thin child with black hair, Jeffrey had rarely shown initiative. Now the questions came in a rush.

"Is the ball metal?" Jeffrey asked.

"Yes," said Miss Lang.

"Is the ring metal?"

"Yes."

"Are the pincers metal?"

"Yes."

"Is the flame hot?"

"Yes."

"Did the ball get hot?"

"Yes."

"Was the ring heated?"

"Yes."

"Was the ball steel?"

"No."

"Copper?"

"No."

"Brass?"

"Yes."

"If the ball got hot enough, would it melt?"

"Yes."

"My theory," Jeffrey said, "is that the ball got fatter."

"Would you like to test your theory?" Miss Lang asked. Jeffrey nodded.

"Did the ball have a chance to cool off?"

"Yes," the teacher said.

"Did the ball get smaller?"

"Yes."

"Did the ring stay almost the same size?"

"Yes."

Jeffrey wildly began waving his hand. "That's it, Miss Lang. That's it." He was grinning now and looking very proud.

As Miss Lang, an enthusiastic first-year teacher, later explained, Jeffrey had solved the problem himself without being forced to make the agonizing choice of announcing before his classmates and teacher a right or wrong theory. Under the SRA program a child may even offer magic as an hypothesis. Eventually as he watches others or participates himself he learns that some theories explain more phenomena and therefore work better than others.

According to Miss Lang, the inquiry method in science has given Jeffrey confidence in himself and as a result has helped him in his reading skills. In the past he was always going to his teacher when he came across a word he did not understand. "Now," said Miss Lang, "he tries to figure out what the words mean himself."

Ultimately the inquiry method should achieve something few textbooks and teachers ever manage to do; it should improve the quality of the questions children ask. If a child learns to ask the right questions, there is nothing he cannot learn.

And yet all these improvements just begin to touch on the increasingly complex problems schools will face in the future. In terms of numbers alone, the nation's grade and high schools will have to educate 73,600,000 children in 1980, almost twice the number going to school now.

"Just to maintain the class ratio of thirty students to one teacher," declared Craig Senft, president of Silver Burdett, "half our college graduates will have to go into teaching by 1970. But lacking the human resources, we will have to turn to technology, to introduce totally new concepts of teaching. We may have to build schools completely run by computers. We may have to build learning rooms in every home where a child sits at a console, presses a button, and retrieves whatever information he needs. We may turn to educational TV and have a master teacher teach a thousand classrooms at once. All these things are technologically possible now. What we don't know is how to use these tools effectively in the teaching process."

And indeed, here lies the problem: what to put in the machines so that they will become effective teachers? It is for this reason that five of the nation's largest electronics manufacturers—Xerox, General Electric, I.B.M., Raytheon, and R.C.A.—have recently acquired or joined forces with publishers who hopefully will supply or supplement the human brain matter that will turn computers into teachers.

The most advanced electronically run educational system

produced to date is the creation of Dr. Patrick C. Suppes, director of Stanford's Institute for Mathematical Studies in the Social Sciences. Dr. Suppes, financed by $2,500,000 in grants from the Carnegie Corporation, the National Science Foundation, and the U. S. Office of Education, has programed an I.B.M. computer which is attempting to teach reading and math to a hundred first graders in East Palo Alto's Brentwood School, where 80 percent of the children are Negro.

The Suppes computer is connected to sixteen student-instruction "terminals" consisting of teletypes, TV screens, and speaker systems. The child sits in a cubicle facing two screens. The screen on his left projects colored slides illustrating concepts or words. The screen before him displays the lessons.

For example, in one reading lesson a child is asked to combine the initial sounds *r,p,* and *b* with the endings *an, at,* and *ag,* and to make *ban, pan, ran, bat, pat, rat, bag,* and *rag.* As each word is flashed on the screen, the youngster, who is also wearing earphones, hears a taped woman's voice pronounce it. Then the voice, always pleasant, always patient, asks the child to touch or write the word *ran* on a cathode-ray tube using an electronic light pen. (He can also respond by typing his answer or by pushing one of several multiple-choice buttons.) If the youngster picks the correct answer, the voice tells him so. If he touches *ban,* then he gets a remedial drill in initial sounds. If he chooses *rag* instead of *ran,* the machine goes over previous lessons because he probably does not understand the lesson being taught.

The Suppes system was first put into use in September, 1966, and it is too early to tell whether it will prove effective. However, if the Suppes programed computer or others like it should work, it could totally revolutionize education in the elementary and high schools and colleges. For the computer possesses within its electronic innards a crucial device which no human being can produce, total and instant recall of all the information that has been fed into it. This means that it eventually and hopefully will be able to serve as an individual instructor which will take into account the strengths and weaknesses of each child. It would do this by modifying the curriculum fed into it on the basis of each student's responses. More drill in the same lesson for one child. A remedial lesson for another. Quick advancement for a third.

At the same time the teacher will be freed from many teaching tasks which a machine might do as well or better and thus will be able to concentrate on those problems which only a human can and probably should handle, whether it be classroom discussion or more individual instruction. Suppes's computer would even give her a print-out containing a complete record of the child's progress for that day. She could then work with the youngster who may have questions the machine is not programed to answer or who still faces problems only a teacher can deal with.

For Dr. Suppes, there must now be "an almost single-minded concentration on individual differences" in the way material is presented to the student. If Dr. Suppes and others achieve this goal, it could hopefully mean the end of the lock-step system of education. The fact that every child has different capabilities is a simplistic observation. Again what is extraordinary is that for the first time large sums of government money and private capital are being invested to see whether there are ways of providing individual instruction for children.

Whether all this will be accomplished depends largely on four factors: money—it costs between $2,000 and $6,000 per student hour to construct a good program, an extraordinarily high sum; time and genius—it took six years for Dr. Suppes and his colleagues to program the Brentwood School math course, which in itself is a remarkable achievement (we are just beginning to learn what learning is all about); and the willingness on the part of the educational establishment to accept innovation.

It is the latter factor, the fear of innovation, that may prove the innovators' biggest hurdle. For not only must the schools accept even more radical change, but teachers and administrators must overcome the humanists' instinctive horror of seeing themselves being replaced by human robots. Fittingly, concern over the recent technological advances was explored by a computer which found itself conversing with a psychiatrist whose conversation appears in lower case. First the psychiatrist speaks:

doctor, i have terrible news
YOU SAY YOU HAVE TERRIBLE NEWS
yes, there is a computer program at m.i.t. that'll ruin us
WHY DO YOU SAY THAT
i have seen it working
YOU SAY YOU HAVE SEEN IT WORKING
it's frightening—you must see it
YOU THINK I MUST SEE IT
we are both in the same boat with respect to that computer
LET'S CONTINUE TO TALK ABOUT YOU—SHALL WE
you are a comfort
WHAT MAKES YOU THINK I AM A COMFORT
at a time like this you want to talk about me
WHY DO YOU THINK I WANT TO TALK ABOUT YOU
because you share my feelings about that damned computer
WHAT DOES THAT SUGGEST TO YOU
that, of course, you hate computers too
YOU THINK I HATE COMPUTERS TOO
why not, they're hardly human, are they
PERHAPS THAT'S WHAT WE ARE HERE TO FIND OUT

no computer could converse as you can, for example
OH
I can't understand how anyone could be fooled by a mere
machine
CAN'T YOU REALLY
for example, could a computer in a conversation like this raise
a new topic
YOU SEEM TO HAVE AVOIDED SPEAKING OF YOUR
PARENTS ALTOGETHER
precisely as you just did
YOU THINK I JUST DID
yes, and that's what shows the difference between a man and
a computer
I SEE

In the new age, not only will a human have to program the
computer and therefore do its original thinking, but once it
has been programed the teacher will have more time to think
and to teach what the computer cannot manage. Moreover,
no machine, however clever its masters, can provide the
inspiration which comes from a human being who himself
is inspired by the subject he loves and the young minds he
is trying to awaken. Finally, no computer with its extraordinary recall, no mass TV class, no self-winding film which a
five-year-old can operate, will ever replace the reading
book, although some of these devices may radically change
the textbook as we have studied it.

"Sadie Zilch in East Overshoe, Iowa, need have no fears,"
declared Craig Senft of Silver Burdett. "All these machines
will free the teacher so that she can give each child more
individual attention. As for the textbook itself, it will always
be with us as long as we are alive. There will always be
something which will serve as the organizational skeleton of
the course. This skeleton may be on a film or series of tapes

or in a single book. As for the students themselves, they will no longer work with just one textbook in each subject. Instead there will be hundreds of books, some in paperback, some in hard cover, some stored on the classroom shelves, others in the school computer. Each book will be different and cover a part of each subject in depth. As Dean Francis Chase of the University of Chicago put it, the biggest revolution in education will come from a better use of books. 'You know,' he said, 'we've never really taken advantage of the printing press.' "

The promise is great. At last, after two hundred years of what must now seem like imperceptible progress, education is finally being touched by the visionaries. In the questions they ask, in the dreams that possess them, they may yet open a world of wonder to the children they seek to teach.

Not long ago Professor Zacharias suggested that since we learn a subject by teaching it ourselves, college students who want to learn about light begin by teaching it to "those golden, glowing ten-year-olds." He suggested many questions both the younger and the older students might ask: "Why are some clouds black? Is the moon white, black, or gray? Can a child find out for himself by asking the moon—not a teacher or a book?"

Someday, in a world beyond the visions of our own prophets, a child may indeed ask the moon.

INDEX

Addison-Wesley, 36-7, 61
Allyn and Bacon, 36, 173-74
American Book Company, 21, 36, 132-36
American Council of Education, 112
American Education Publications, 35
American Institute of Biological Sciences, 139
Anderson, Astrid C., 97, 116
Appleton and Company, 82, 83-4
Armitage, Russell, 54-5

Bankston, Hubert S., 144
Barr, Donald, 148
Bennion, Grant, 41, 137
Biological Sciences Curriculum Study (BSCS), 139-45, 153-61

Book trust, 132-38
Brackman, Walter, 12-4
Brandwein, Paul, 165
Brown, Fay, 156, 158
Bruner, Dr. Jerome, 138
Bunge, William, 97
Burney, King, 150-52
Byerly, Dr. Carl, 113, 122-23

Cason, Jack, 146-47
Catholic textbooks, 78-9
Chauncey, Henry, 165
Controversial Material. See Racial bias; Religious bias; Communism, 101-4; evolution, 18, 80-1, 143-45, 153-60; McCarthyism, 95, 153; pro-Americanism, 88-90, 97-105, 160-61; sex, 19-22, 142-43; survey of teaching of, 91-5; temperance, 89-90; United Nations, 149-50, 153

A Note About the Author

Hillel Black was born and raised in New York City, and received his M.A. from the University of Chicago in English and foreign languages. He began his career as a journalist in 1952, working for *The New York Times*. He also worked and wrote for The Associated Press and CBS. He was an editor of *The Saturday Evening Post* for several years before becoming a Senior Editor for William Morrow. Mr. Black is the author of *They Shall Not Pass, The Watchdogs of Wall Street, Buy Now, Pay Later,* and co-author of *The Thief in the White Collar* and *The Royal Vultures.*